THE dang FACTOR

A No-Nonsense Lesson
on Life and Love

THE dang FACTOR

MICHELLE
AFONT

The anecdotes and advice herein are not intended to replace the services of trained mental health professionals. You are advised to consult with your health-care professional with regard to matters relating to your mental health, and in particular, regarding matters that may require diagnosis or medical attention. The author and publisher specifically disclaim any liability that is incurred from the use or application of the contents of this book.

The names and identifying characteristics of some of the individuals featured throughout this book have been changed to protect their privacy. Any resemblance to actual persons, living or dead, is purely coincidental.

TFS PRESS

P.O. Box 7172
Stateline, NV 89449
TFSPress.com

Book Design by Monkey C Media, monkeyCmedia.com
Author Photo by Chad Thompson, ChadThompsonPhotography.com

Printed in the United States of America
First Edition

ISBN: 978-0-9988630-6-1 (trade paperback)
978-0-9988630-2-3 (eBook)
978-0-9988630-3-0 (ePub)

Library of Congress Control Number: 2017911781

The Dang Factor is dedicated to *all* women of the world, regardless of age, sexual orientation, location, or status. Change the way you love and love the way you change.

—Michelle

Dang

/dæŋ/

Noun

1. A person toward whom you feel intense affection and a sexual attraction.
2. A partner whom you love to be around and whom you miss when gone.
3. Someone you look at who causes you to think to yourself, DANG! You dig him! You think he is hot. You admire him. You respect him. You love his touch and want to be close to him.
4. A partner who makes your vagina tingle.

Verb

1. To share your life with a partner whom you adore and sexually desire.
2. To really dig the person you are with.
3. The little bit of pitter that continues to patter in your relationship.

ORIGIN: a beach in Del Mar, California

The Dang Factor will:

Inspire you. Motivate you. Empower you. Change you.

- ✓ If you are single
- ✓ If you are dating
- ✓ If you and your partner no longer share the same life goals
- ✓ If your goal is to be married
- ✓ If your goal is motherhood
- ✓ If you have doubts about commitment
- ✓ If you are not sure that he is your Dang
- ✓ If you are married and he has never been your Dang
- ✓ If you are married and he was once your Dang but now, eh, not so much
- ✓ If you've never experienced real, passionate, mutually adoring love
- ✓ If you cringe at the thought of sex with your partner
- ✓ If you have been auditioning for the role of wife for far too long
- ✓ If your vagina used to tingle when he touched you but has gone into hibernation
- ✓ If your vagina has *never* tingled when he touched you
- ✓ If you would *love* for your vagina to tingle when he touches you
- ✓ If you want to re-create the passion you once shared
- ✓ If you want to save your marriage because it has one morsel of Dang still there
- ✓ If you have outgrown your current relationship
- ✓ If your future deathbed is missing an essential piece of your life puzzle
- ✓ If you are ready to crack the code to damn good love

Contents

Preface

Several years ago, I watched helplessly as my father lay on his deathbed and weakly told me he was not ready to die. As I held his hand, he told me he had never experienced love during his lifetime. Not just "love" as the word is so freely used, but that real, passionate, rock-your-world kind of love. My father whispered to me his many regrets as we sat together during his last twenty-four hours of life.

As he spoke, I saw my future self, lying on my deathbed, with the same sad regrets. Although I was in my twenty-fifth year of marriage, I too had never really felt passionate love.

My father died the following day, and my world forever changed. His death breathed life into me. My twenty-five-year marriage was the only world I had known, but with the help of my father, I was finally able to step *outside* of my life and look *inside* at my life. My forty-four-year-old self did not like what she saw. I made the decision to rearrange my deathbed while I still had time. I left my marriage and journeyed into a world unknown. My five-year quest to find real love brought *The Dang Factor* to life.

The Dang Factor is a book about changing the way women love. It is about learning to un-love when a relationship does not go as planned. *The Dang Factor* is a main course of empowerment with a side dish of accountability. It is about inspiring and motivating women everywhere to evaluate the state of their love lives and make the changes necessary to find, restore, and keep passionate and mutual love in their lives. It is about helping women to steer their own ships into their personal harbors of happiness. It is about looking *in* so you can finally look *out* at the life you choose. It is about bringing the almighty lust back into your life and reviving your self-love. It is about lessons on leaving a love that is not well suited to you and nurturing a love that is.

It is about taking stock in *you*. It is about settling for no less than adoring and reciprocated love from your partner. It is about being fortunate enough to have the opportunity to disassemble and rearrange your life to suit and satisfy *you*.

Introduction

The Dang Factor is a lesson on life and love. Seeking it. Finding it. Losing it. Keeping it. Nurturing it. *The Dang Factor* is your guide to not missing out on the greatest emotion you will ever feel. It was written out of my love for women and my desire to give women the strength to love well. In order to strengthen you, I must be candid with you. I may occasionally hit a nerve. You may not like me at times. And that's okay. I did not write *The Dang Factor* in an effort to be liked. I wrote it because I never, ever want you to give up on the joy of love you so richly deserve.

Little did I know my five-year journey to discover the deepest love imaginable not only would lead me to my "Dang," but also would inspire my mission to empower women to seek and live a love- and sex-soaked life.

The Dang Factor is your tool to motivate you to look in at your life and honestly access the status of your life objectives. This book is about igniting a change in you—and the way you live and love your way through life. *The Dang Factor* will inspire you to steer your own vessel into the port of satisfying love and *mutually* enjoyable sex.

I did not write *The Dang Factor* to encourage the breakup of your current relationship. Instead, *The Dang Factor* asks you to take a hard look at what is and isn't working in your relationships. Along the way, we will talk about how to find love with a partner you physically crave. We will assess your sexual attraction to your current partner. We will knock down the roadblocks that are keeping you from a fulfilling partnership. We will talk about how to reignite the sexual spark within you. We will explore dating, marriage, sex, betrayal, breakups, makeups, and, most importantly, the relaunch of good love in your life.

I know the Dang Life because I live the Dang Life. I had to work like hell to find it. And I work even harder to keep it. To find a love I had never had, I needed to do something I had never done. I switched up and rearranged my own deathbed to search for what was missing in my life. I took a chance. I paid my dues. I put the time in. I have felt the depths of fear and the agonizing pain of loss along the way.

My journey to love was not easy, but it was necessary. I got down in the ditches and searched for what I wanted out of life. I live what I nag. I breathe what I bitch. I am a success story of love, and my mission is to make *mutual* and lasting love a reality for you too.

Although *The Dang Factor* is a book written for women, men will be equally absorbed by its powerful and straightforward message. To complement The Dang Factor, men of all ages will find my simple message to them in *The Dude Factor: A Man's Guide to The Dang Factor.*

1

Death can dish out life.

My Deathbed

We are all going to die. It is the only guarantee we have in life. The question is, what is that moment going to be like for you?

Death isn't an easy topic to discuss. Many prefer to keep their heads buried in the sand until faced with their final moments. But I believe those who are willing to look death straight in the eye ultimately live the fullest lives. If your life were to end tomorrow, what would your deathbed feel like? Would it be regretful? Would you be surrounded by love? Would you meet your final moments with satisfaction at the depth of the love you received and felt with your partner?

Some people die quickly and unexpectedly, robbed of the chance to reflect on their lives. Others are made aware of their impending death and have the opportunity to look back on the lives they have lived. Still others are given many years to think ahead to their final moments. These years are a gift, unparalleled opportunities to reflect upon their lives and make changes before their deaths.

On your deathbed, there are no go-backs. No do-overs. No more chances. If you know me, you know about my deathbed scenario. It is a moment I try to envision on a daily basis. Certainly not because I think about the event of death itself, but rather because I envision the mindset and reflection I will have when that moment comes. My goal, of course, is to meet the end of my life knowing I have lived a life filled with deep and adoring love, meaningful adventure, and indescribable memories.

For me, the realization of finality and looking back at my life came as I held my father's hand as he lay on his deathbed.

My father was a young sixty-five years old when he was diagnosed with terminal lung cancer. He was the epitome of positivity, jovial and upbeat all the time. I would never have known of his deathbed regrets had he not shared them with me during his last twenty-four hours of life.

Whether he wasn't able to accept his diagnosis or he was protecting me, I'll never know. I just remember my sister called and said we needed to go see Dad. On our flight from

San Diego to his hospital in Sacramento, I had no idea what to expect.

We landed and drove straight to the hospital. I can still see the room clearly. There were two beds. One was empty, and the other had a man sitting upright in a hospital gown. I walked in, looked straight at the stranger, and walked out. I found a nurse and said, "Hi, I'm looking for my dad." She said, "Oh, honey, you were just in there with him."

I had not even recognized my own father.

My dad had been a jolly and rotund character the last time I'd seen him, not more than a year ago. Now, he was a shell of his former self.

"Hi, Honey," he weakly whispered.

"Hi, Dad." I grabbed his hand, once plump and sturdy, now just skin and bones.

As I was trying to take in the surprise of his physical condition, my dad hit me with an even bigger bombshell.

"I'm not ready to die. I have so many regrets. I have never felt love."

As I stroked his hand, trying to provide comfort, he kept repeating the same mantra. "I need just a little more time. I want to feel what love feels like." He kept whispering these same regrets while I helplessly said, "It's going to be all right."

But it wasn't.

Sure, he'd loved his children and grandchildren. But he had gone his entire life without experiencing true, all-consuming, romantic love. He sadly spoke of the missing links. Of empty love and his wish that his family could be together to share magical memories that were never made.

"I'm not ready. I don't want to die. I'm not ready. I don't want to die," he repeated over and over.

My father was not ready to leave this world—not with so many dreams and adventures unfulfilled. He wanted more time to find and embrace a deeper love before he died. He wanted his deathbed moment to be peaceful and beautiful, knowing he had lived and loved life to the fullest.

I could not fathom that this was how life ends. *This is it?*

His regrets were more shocking than his declining body. These never-mentioned, never-questioned, never-shared regrets about a life lived without love consumed his last hours.

The whole picture sent shockwaves of disbelief through my body. *This is the way it ends?*

Life offers us this fantastic opportunity to find love, build a life with a partner, have a fulfilling relationship, and finish our time on Earth with peace. My father felt none of this. Only the regrets of a life lived without love. These were what ruminated in his mind. Regrets. Asking for time, when the time for action had long passed.

He had so much love to give and wished he had made finding real love a priority in his life. My father died the following day, and my world changed forever.

I was taken aback at the complete finality and sad passing of my father. I remember going out into the hospital hallway and breaking down. I wondered out loud, "How can this be?" How can someone live life in a humdrum bubble without change and adventure? How can a person live life settling for a relationship void of love and desire? How can someone just coast through life and not savor and seek out adoring love and magnetic sex?

I could not fathom how one could paddle through the opportunity of life and, at the end, have so many regrets. It was so sad to watch my father look back at his life and speak of the missing link he craved, yet never found.

Witnessing my father's death awakened me. Although I was in my twenty-fifth year of marriage, I realized I too had never experienced deep and passionate love. As if a blaring alarm clock began to ring incessantly, I received a wake-up call from my dad that told me to make changes in my life so that my own deathbed would not mimic my father's.

That one moment in time changed my life forever. Feeling like I'd been kicked in the gut, I looked in at my deathbed. Sadly, I saw myself lying there with the same regrets and unfulfilled dreams as my father's. I was mortified by the thought of my life ending as my father's had.

Generally speaking, my impending deathbed looked relatively peaceful. I'd been married to the same man for twenty-five years. I had four fabulous children, whom I adored. I'd finished my education and had obtained my law degree. I had a career as a successful attorney and life advisor. I had an incredible family and a close circle of friends. But with all of the incredible in my life, something was missing. Something was terribly wrong with my life, and I needed to fix it.

In my heart, I knew what was missing: I was not in love. Sure, I was married, but I was not in love. Don't get me wrong; I did love my husband. However, I loved him as I would love my brother. Passionate love? Not a chance. Real love? Not even close. Lust for my man? Hell no. In fact, I had never been in love. My father's passing led me to realize the simple truth about my life: I was missing the same link to love that my father was missing on his deathbed.

Had my father not died before my eyes in the manner he did, I am convinced I would have stayed in my loveless marriage forever. I would have plugged away each day just going through the motions of married life. I would have continued to do what I was comfortable doing. My fear of the unknown would have outweighed my desire for happiness.

But witnessing my father's death set off a spark within me. Like a bolt of lightning, his death propelled me to envision my deathbed and seek out the missing piece of my life puzzle.

It may sound odd, but as my father took his last breath, he breathed new life into me.

On my deathbed, I wanted to have no regrets. I did not want to lie there, as my father had, and wish I could have done better things with my life. Although cliché, it finally dawned on me: I get one chance at this life of mine. I was forty-four years old and could already picture myself lying on my deathbed, regretting the fact that I had never experienced the one thing missing in my life: *LOVE*.

I don't mean brotherly or humdrum love. I am talking about *LOVE*. Real love. Passionate love. The kind of love you feel to your toes. A love so incredible it makes you weak in the knees. Could this type of love really exist? If so, I knew I needed to try to find it and savor every single second of it.

Now that I had pinpointed my impending deathbed issue, I set out to fix it and change my life. Luckily, I had something my father did not: I had *time* to make some changes in my life.

So I made a change, right there in the hospital lobby. My father passed, and two minutes later I called my husband.

"We need to talk when I get back from the funeral. Will you pick me up at the airport?"

My husband knew from the call: I was out, and our marriage was done. The missing link of my life could not be fixed by staying together. One minute I was married, and then the next it was over. I didn't think. It was an instinctual, instantaneous moment.

Ending my twenty-five-year marriage was the quickest decision I had ever made. I didn't know the *how* or *what next,* but I had to get out. I didn't weigh my options; I didn't care. If I had to work five jobs, that was all right. I was willing to do anything not to die the same death as my dad. The details didn't matter.

I took the scene of what happened to my father, and then, within two minutes, I created a new scene for my life.

My father gave me a priceless gift the day he died. He taught me life's biggest lesson: To have a life without regrets, you must live life to the fullest and love to the deepest. His final gift to me was his greatest. It's the hardest lesson I have had to learn and one that has changed my life for the better in countless, beautiful ways.

2

It is okay to leave an unconnected love. It is the manner of exit that will set the skyline of your future.

Lessons on Leaving

Without shedding a tear, I walked away from my quarter-of-a-century marriage. There was not one ounce of sadness in me. In essence, I had checked out of my marriage many years before. I knew, without a doubt, that taking this next step in my life was the right thing to do. I had given my marriage twenty-five years to *feel* different to me, but it was time to move forward.

So I switched up my life. I disassembled my life. I rearranged my life. I did not know how or where I would find this elusive love, but I knew it was out there and that if I did not look for it, it would never be felt.

Now, I want to give you a little background. My ex-husband of twenty-five years is a sweet and caring man. I don't think we ever had a single fight in all of our years together. He never raised his voice to me. Every Friday, without fail, he brought me flowers.

This man did nothing *wrong* as a husband. He was devoted to me and was always a perfect gentleman. He was a hard worker and did his best to provide for our family. I am convinced he would never have ended our marriage. He was content to live two very separate lives as husband and wife.

Our problem was a common one: We had grown in different directions. I have always felt there should be forward momentum over the years whereby each partner improves and grows in some way. After we got married at the age of twenty, I naturally assumed we would move on from our jobs at the local lumber company.

Over the next twenty-five years, I grew as a person. I returned to school and obtained my bachelor's degree. I went on to attend law school and received my juris doctor degree. I loved the idea of education and self-betterment.

On the opposite spectrum, my husband was content with the status quo. I encouraged him to return to school, but he had no desire. This is not meant to put him down. This is just who he is. I am driven. He's content with a simpler life.

Our interests and pursuits started to diverge. We began living separate lives. Our only mutual interest was our four children. Now, some forty years later, he's still at the same lumber company, where he works as a truck driver. For our marriage to have had a chance to survive, my husband needed to grow with me and evolve from the state of mind we had when we were both twenty years old.

After my moment of enlightenment with my father's death, I realized I needed more in my marriage and my life. I craved more than just going through the motions of marriage and existing in a roommate-like state of mind with my husband.

My Marriage Mantra

During my marriage, I lived by a personal mantra: *Love your children more than you love yourself.* I repeated this phrase to myself multiple times a day. Every day. For twenty-five years.

The thought of divorce never entered my mind. I reminded myself that it was *I* who chose to marry at a young age. *I* was the one who made a choice to have children and start a family at the age of twenty. *I* was the one who needed to see my marriage through until the end: *'til death do us part.*

So my children became my life. Divorce was not an option. I came from a divorced family and vowed to stay married "for the sake of the children." So I faked it. I threw myself into being a mother to our four children, a role I embraced. My life was defined by my role as a mother. I acted like a mother. I associated with other mothers. My life revolved around my children's sporting events and activities.

I was a mother, but I never felt like a wife.

My role as a lover never existed in my marriage. I had no desire to be in an intimate and passionate relationship with my husband. The truth was, I was not physically attracted to him the way I should have been. I used to dread hearing his car pull into the garage because I knew he would want to kiss me when he came through the door. I often wondered what was wrong with me. Why did I have no sexual desire for my husband? After years of wondering, I finally resolved my lack of sexual desire and convinced myself I must not be "wired" for sex.

I had never loved my husband in a romantic way. For crying out loud, I was a twenty-year-old when I married him. My brain was not even fully developed. My husband was a sort of brother or pal. There was no way I could love him or want him in any impassioned way.

In my silly mind, I thought that as time went on I would *want him* and have feelings for him the way a wife was *supposed* to. Having four children together did not bring those feelings. Building our dream home did not bring those feelings. Buying a new car did not bring those feelings. Graduating from law school did not bring those feelings. Ultimately, I ran out of ways to try to make love happen. No matter what I did, I couldn't conjure the feelings missing in my marriage.

A New Mantra Emerges

After my father passed, my entire thought process changed. I questioned everything about my life and my happiness. My deathbed continued to flash in my mind like a neon street sign. At that point in my life, my deathbed moment seemed so sad, as if something magnificent was missing.

Was something wrong with me? If so, then why were so many people I knew stuck in the same loveless and sexless trap? So many couples I knew lived in the same robotic-like state that never varied from day to day. No outward affection, no physical connection. Couples with nothing in common except their children. No sexy getaways or time carved out to savor each other. Date nights that never seemed to happen. Promises of closeness that never materialized. Excuses. Always excuses.

How were these couples not going crazy? Did they think this was all life offered? Didn't they want more? Didn't they know their lives were set for forward motion only? No rewinds. No go-backs. No do-overs. It made me crazy as I looked around at how detached some people were in their marriages.

In a moment that made me stop in my tracks, I thought, *What am I teaching my children?* When I thought about the message I was sending to my children, I was taken aback.

To love my children more than I love myself was a silly and misguided mantra.

What Should We Really Teach Our Children?

The thought that my children could end up in a marriage like mine sickened me. What, indeed, was I teaching them? That a decision they made at twenty was something they must honor for life? No! I finally realized I was setting the wrong example for my children by sticking it out in a marriage void of mutual love and adoration.

I came to understand that the idea of "staying together for the children" was nothing but a bunch of crap. Sure, ideally, a two-parent family is wonderful. But two parents who aren't in love, avoid intimacy, and have absolutely nothing in common need not sacrifice their lives and happiness for the sake of the children.

I knew my children would be okay. In fact, I knew they would thrive when I ended my marriage to their father. I knew this because of what I was *about* to teach them.

Lessons on Leaving

When I made my decision to end my marriage, our four children were eight, ten, nineteen, and twenty-two years old. We decided to sit all the children down as a group and tell them we would be getting a divorce. During my speech to the children, I made it clear that no one had done anything wrong.

I explained to them that sometimes people marry for the wrong reasons or they simply evolve into different people along the way. I explained—and meant it—that we truly cared for each other. Our lives had just taken different paths over the past twenty-five years.

To be honest, our eight- and ten-year-olds were barely fazed. This is not to say they were not affected in some way. But if you ask them now, as adults, they will tell you they had an incredible childhood filled with love and happiness, in spite of being children of divorce. Because of our presentation and maturity, they took our lead. Children are very resilient. In my experience, it's when the parents set out to destroy one another and turn into enemies that children fall apart and carry that scarring over into their adult years.

As a divorce attorney for more than twenty years, I have seen firsthand the way many parents conduct themselves during a divorce. It is not pretty, and some parents should be ashamed of what they have burdened their children with. I vowed I would never conduct myself in that manner, nor would I ever subject my children to any negative talk about their father.

I have always been intrigued by how people conduct themselves following a breakup. Over the years, I've learned not only that people's character is measured by the way they conduct themselves *during* a relationship, but also, the measure of character is the way they conduct themselves *after* the relationship ends.

The breakup of our marriage had nothing to do with my husband. It had to do with me, and what I was seeking in my pre-deathbed life. I was not out to destroy him. I was not out to ruin him. I wanted him to be happy and have a wonderful life. I wanted him to meet a lovely woman along the way and remarry. We both agreed the children would remain our priority. It was the one joint responsibility that our divorce could not diminish.

My soon-to-be-ex did not move out of our family home immediately. Instead, he moved into our spare room. In the meantime, I purchased several large moving boxes and placed them in our living room. Each box was labeled "Daddy's House." We had the children pick several of their favorite things to put in the boxes: beloved stuffed animals, blankets, games, toys, and clothes. Each time we'd go shopping, they picked out a few new things to put in their "Daddy Box."

Over the course of the next couple of months, they had amassed quite a collection of new toys and special items for when they were at Daddy's house. Of course, they were not allowed to open or play with any of their new treasures until Dad made the move to his new home. As I write this, I cannot help but chuckle at the memory of the overflowing boxes in our living room. Finally, after gathering their "Dad Treasures" over several months, they were begging their dad to hurry up and move already. They were anxious to begin their life at Dad's place half time (and start playing with a few new Barbies as well).

As for our adult children, their reactions were each very different. Our nineteen-year-old daughter was not surprised in the slightest. It was evident to her that I had been unfulfilled for some time. She was more surprised that we'd stayed together for so long. She elaborated by adding we had absolutely nothing in common and basically had lived two separate lives for as long as she could remember. She was right, of course, but I was a bit taken aback by her insight.

Our adult son was a different matter altogether. Initially, he was very upset with me. He prided himself on the fact that of all his friends, his parents were one of the few couples still married. I firmly explained to my son that this was *my* life. While he was off to college, having the time of his life and dating up a storm, how could he possibly want me to sit home with his father and be miserable, just for the sake of being able to tell his friends his parents were still married?

I stood my ground. I expected him to respect my decision—not support my decision, mind you, but to respect it. I also let him know that if he would like to move back to our home and spend each night in our marriage (since he thought our marriage was so great), he needed to do just that. I cautioned him not to look in from the outside and pretend to know our marriage.

No one knows anyone else's marriage. Trust me on that. Within a short time, my son realized how unhappy I had been. As I started my journey into my new life, my son watched me blossom and burst with excitement about my new adventures. Ultimately, he became one of my biggest supporters. I had come alive, and it felt damn good.

Instead of teaching my children to stick it out in an unfulfilling and depressing relationship or situation in life, I have taught my children to make the necessary changes in their lives to achieve the things they crave and deserve. More importantly, I taught them to make changes with dignity, kindness, and class. I taught my children that sometimes relationships end. Friendships end. Jobs end. People often do not grow together or forge the same paths in life. And that's okay. I taught my children it is the manner in which you walk away from an unsatisfying situation that will determine your character and set the scene for your future.

With my deathbed reevaluated and redirected, I began my unknown journey to try to find the missing piece of my life puzzle. During my five-year quest to find love, I gained an abundance of insight and experience that I'm thrilled to share with you in *The Dang Factor*. Happily, the missing piece was found and slid perfectly into my life's puzzle. I now know what love is. Real love. Adoring love. A feel-it-to-my-toes kind of love. And ten years later, I still feel it. As of today, I am happy to report my deathbed is looking pretty damned satisfying.

12 Lessons on Leaving

1. *Do* be civil. I know it can be tough to be pleasant when a relationship ends, but your breakup attitude will set the entire scene for your future.

2. *Do* take responsibility for any role you may have played in the breakup. Learn and grow from your missteps of love.

3. *Do* focus on the *good* that came out of the relationship.

4. *Do* accept the fact that *something* was broken in your relationship. Devoted couples do not break up. For a relationship to work, both parties must be *equally* committed and smitten with each other.

5. *Do* get excited about your future. Your future is now a blank white canvas, and *you* get to paint the picture.

6. *Do not* wallow in what "was." What *was* in the past was apparently not working. Stay focused on what "is," as in, "Your future *is* going to be amazing."

7. *Do not* obsess on the reasons for the breakup. *Use the reasons* as a spark for reflection and self-betterment.

8. *Do* be dignified. Be fair and reasonable in the division of any assets.

9. *Do not* wish him a lifetime of unhappiness. That serves no purpose other than to keep your life from moving forward in a positive and productive way.

10. *Do* resist the urge to talk about him. You could end up getting back together with him, so there's no need to publicize his faults.

11. *Do* wish him well and mean it. Not all relationships will last a lifetime. Use this newfound time in your life to rebirth yourself and emerge as a stronger and self-loving woman.

12. *Do* love your children more than you dislike their father. Parental alienation is real and causes permanent damage to children. Trust me, I know rising above his behavior is not always easy, but for the sake of *your* future and that of your children, make every effort to be the bigger person. Your attitude will determine your children's altitude, as they soar to reach great heights throughout their life.

3

It's the uncovered phenomenon for sex and relationship longevity.

The Dang Factor

The Dang Factor is the most important chapter of this book. Why? It's simple: Either you Dang or you don't. The Dang Factor is the crux of your future love, sex, lust, partnership, and all around blissful life. If your deathbed is looking a tad bleak because you've never felt the deep and unbelievable love that you deserve, listen up. Your journey to adoring love hinges on *your* Dang Factor, and trust me when I say *what a difference a Dang makes!*

The concept of the Dang Factor originated on the beach in Del Mar, California. On a warm July day, I was spending the day with my then-sixteen-year-old daughter and a few of her girlfriends. At the time, my daughter, Tristen, had recently started her first boyfriend relationship. As Tristen stood on the beach next to me, I couldn't help but notice her head spinning side to side as each surfer boy strode by with his tanned body and salty blond hair.

"Tristen, why are you drooling over all of these boys?"

"Because they are so cute, Mom."

"Tristen!" I shot back. "You have a boyfriend."

"Yes, Mom," Tristen said. "But I want a boyfriend who, when he walks into the room, I say, '*Dang!*'"

And there it was. That moment of enlightenment was born. "The Dang Factor" became the dating bar that all new suitors in our family needed to achieve. The question perpetually asked among our family became, "Does he/she meet the Dang Factor?"

As time went by, I started to observe how many couples I knew who were truly each other's Dang. You know the couples who are crazy about each other and not afraid to show it. The enthusiastic love they feel for each other radiates off them. I observed couples who had been married for twenty-plus years and still couldn't keep their hands off each other.

You can spot them a mile away. There are holding hands over the table. They are enjoying the same passions and hobbies. They touch each other. They play together. Their life together is loving and sexual. Their life as a couple did not get swallowed up when the children came along. They call each other sweet terms of endearment. They genuinely like each other. A lot.

Sadly, however, many relationships are the complete opposite. We have all seen these couples. They are the ones at a restaurant who are sitting together but not speaking. They are the couples who put each other down with jarring insults. They are the couples who live two separate lives—each doing his or her own thing, but doing nothing together.

They are the couples who never touch. Never kiss. Never say, "I love you." They are the couples who merely coexist for the sake of being a couple for fear of being alone. They are the couples who pretend to the world to be happy. But behind closed doors, they are simply going through the motions of an unemotional coexistence.

What Exactly Is a Dang?

A Dang is a partner who turns you on. A Dang is a partner you love to be around and miss when gone. A Dang is that little bit of pitter that continues to patter. It's a little bit of lust that continues to loom. And most importantly, your Dang is someone you look at who causes you to think to yourself, *DANG!* You dig him. You think he is hot. You admire him. You respect him. You love to touch him. And you want to have sex with him.

Quite simply, to quote my dear friend, Stella, "He makes my vagina tingle." Although Stella's interpretation of her Dang made me laugh, she was spot on. Your Dang is a partner who does indeed make your vagina tingle and come alive.

A Dang comes in every shape, size, and color. What may be one woman's Dang may not be yours. Your Dang is unique to *you*. Only you can know what it is about him that Dangs you.

Do not make the mistake of thinking your desired partner has to have ripped, eight-pack abs. Don't get hung up thinking your partner needs to have the perfect body or features. Don't get stuck thinking he or she needs the perfect career or an incredible income. The person you love does not need to come from a picture-perfect family or drive a fancy car. No one is ever going to be perfect. What matters is that your partner is ideally suited to be with *you*.

You may be attracted to your ideal partner because of his intellect, sense of humor, compassion, or ambition. Maybe his passion, personality, or philanthropy interests attract you. Whatever it is, it's there. You cannot fake it. Either you Dang, or you don't. There is no gray area of Dang.

However, your attraction to someone *can* grow over time. It does not need to be Dang at first sight. Sometimes it simply takes a bit of time to figure out real love. I did not feel love at first sight with my second husband. It took a few dates to get me there, but when I did, it was incredible.

Without the Dang Factor present in your relationship, you will be missing the most incredible feeling you could ever experience: raw, powerful, I-need-to-touch-this-person kind of love.

The Relationship Glue

It is that mountain of Dang that keeps a couple together through thick and thin. In essence, it's that incredible helping of attraction that keeps you from walking away. That little bit of Dang is the glue that keeps the relationship strong, despite being tested.

My life is not perfect by any means. My husband and I are not immune to the many curveballs of life. Although deeply in love, we argue and disagree (a lot), as most couples do. Sometimes, I cannot stand him. And vice versa. We've had our share of relationship low points. At times, our lows were so low that many people would have walked away. And during those lows, not one morsel of me considered permanently walking away.

Not because I'm comfortable. Not because I'm scared to be alone. Not because I've already been through one divorce. I stay because he is "The One" for me. And through it all, at the end of the issue, or the argument we just had, or the night one of us slept on the couch, I eventually still want to touch him and have him as my life partner.

That feeling of *Dang* is the reason we stay in what would otherwise be a relationship we would terminate in a heartbeat. It's that slice of attraction that propels us to work through the imperfections and indiscretions of our partners and tolerate the occasional jerks they can be. That piece of yearning is the motivation to work day in and day out on our relationship and fight like hell to stay committed as a couple.

From Dang to Un-Dang

What once was your Dang could easily turn into your un-Dang. Your partner needs to "check your boxes" in a majority of aspects of your life. You have to be sparked on all cylinders: physically, emotionally, and spiritually.

How does someone get un-Danged? Easy. Your partner can lose status by his or her behavior over a period of time. Her pretty eyes or his kind demeanor might initially attract you, but over time, the status can change.

My friend Sandy is a perfect example. Sandy and James were crazy about each other. They dated for three years, and Sandy assumed they would eventually marry. But when James waged a bitter custody war against his ex-wife, James lost his Dang status in Sandy's eyes. Sandy was so turned off by his spiteful behavior that she promptly ended their three-year relationship.

Similarly, lack of effort in the relationship, laziness, lack of ambition, and nastiness from either partner can propel a Dang into an un-Dang. Infidelity, lack of respect for your relationship, or any abuse is sure to lead to an un-Dang status.

To men, finding the perfect partner is rather simple: physical attraction rates as the number one criterion to attract a man. For women, however, our criteria run deeper. For women, a good majority of our attraction to our partner is gained by his actions. In other words, your guy can look like Channing Tatum, but if he's an asshole, you are not going to want to be with him.

A woman's attraction to her partner evolves from a respectful, nurturing, kind, generous, and helpful kind of guy. In essence, women have a two-step process they need to complete to reach a preferred level of attraction. Physical attraction is, of course, step one. Step two is where the nurturing takes over. Do the dishes, make dinner, watch the kids, or rub our feet, and it's on. When men nurture our souls, they feed our level of attraction to them.

Relationships take work, effort, and communication. Maintaining mutual love and attraction does not just magically happen. I can assure you that each marriage that takes place does not happen with the idea of eventually falling out of love. Actions and behaviors can happen along the way that may cause a relationship to become unhinged and un-Danged (hence, the over-50percent divorce rate).

Be Dang Smart

Caution: Your Dang can be a blessing or a curse. Your partner is a curse if you waste too much of your life on a person who is a certified ass, a legitimate jerk, or not a stand-up person. He is a curse if the love and attraction you feel toward him are not reciprocal. He is a curse if you are marriage-and child-minded and he has no intention of making a commitment, marrying you, or starting a family with you.

Remember, the attraction has to work in both directions. The lure cannot be one-sided, felt only by you. Your partner needs to feel the pull equally, if not more than you. Do not waste your time on someone who does not unequivocally think of you as his "I cannot live without this person in my life" kind of woman.

He is a curse if the two of you do not share the same life goals, needs, and desires. I want you to be able to recognize when you are not being wise in your relationship choices. I want you to force yourself to step outside of yourself and look in at *your* life. Do not let his overwhelming hotness cloud your good judgment.

Keep your life and love goals in focus. Do you want to be married? Do you want to become a mother? Do you want to find a partner you sexually desire and adore? Do *you* want to be sexually desired and adored?

Don't be afraid to move forward with your life by making some positive changes. Your reality is simple: You don't have the luxury to give away years of your life to someone and still reach the goals you wish to achieve. You must be cautious of the way you choose to spend your time. You just have this *one* lifetime. Don't fritter it away on a partner if one or more of the following statements are true:

He is not your Dang.

You are not his Dang.

Your life and relationship goals do not match up.

Granite Will Not Fix It

As women, when it comes to relationships, we often find ourselves in an all-or-nothing state of mind. After we have made a commitment, most women tend to be committed to the relationship 110 percent. We tend to dive headfirst into love and give our partners every ounce of our beings. When that enlightened moment arrives, when we realize that our relationship may not be the right one, instead of leaving the relationship, we tend to place Band-Aids on the festering love. We try to mend the broken aspects of the relationship and subconsciously hope for a magical fix.

For me, that moment of enlightenment came right after I got married for the first time. Before my marriage, the idea of a wedding and a fun reception intrigued me. After all, isn't it every girl's dream to have a big wedding and be the bride? Although my first husband was certainly not the love of my life, I thought that as soon as we became "husband and wife," I would magically become sexually attracted to him. I talked myself into believing that once we were married, I would crave him as a sexual partner. I thought that after we said, "I do," I would want him and feel the way I was *supposed* to feel about my new husband.

After our wedding, I waited for that *magical* transformation to happen. Suffice it to say the magic never materialized. Being married didn't make me crave my new husband. Again, he was a nice person; he simply wasn't my Dang. Soon after the wedding, I knew my husband would never make me go weak in the knees. I would never feel the "butterflies" in my stomach I'd heard so much about.

If you are in a relationship or marriage and you find yourself Dang-less and uninspired, you have probably done what most women do to make discontent more tolerable: We buy things. We build things. We find distractions. We do all that we can to distract from the reality that our union is mundane, robotic, sexless, routine, and without some serious attraction for one another.

We may install new granite countertops in the kitchen, hoping they will fix the relationship problems. But ultimately, the granite does not fix it. The granite was merely a Band-Aid used as a distraction until the thrill of the new countertops wore off.

The relationship fix-it is not limited to granite. It's getting a new puppy. It's having another baby. It's rearranging the furniture for the umpteenth time. It's hours spent on Pinterest planning the perfect Halloween party. It is anything other than facing the harsh reality of the unsatisfying state of our relationships.

My neighbor bought a convertible BMW sports car when she could no longer fake her marriage. She and her husband spent months researching and test-driving sports cars to find the right "fix" for their marriage. Needless to say, the BMW did not fix the marriage.

Another friend moved with her husband to Italy for a "fresh start." As you can guess, Italy did not fix her marriage. The same Dang-less problem only followed them to Italy. Same shitty marriage, different postal code.

Bottom line: granite (the children, the dog, the new paint) will not fix it.

Without the Dang Factor in your relationship, granite does not fix it. All of the money and material possessions in the world cannot make your marginal dude into your Dang.

I used one distraction after another to keep my focus off of my brother/sister type of marriage. I knew right away I'd made a mistake getting married so young, so I found distractions to get me through the next twenty-five years of marriage. My four children were an enormous piece of granite that ultimately did not fix my marriage. I loved being a mother, but that didn't fix my marriage.

I also went back to school and obtained my bachelor's degree (another distraction). After that, I enrolled in law school, which distracted me for another three years.

By the time my father passed, I had run out of distractions. Four children, two degrees, three houses, and two dogs later, the truth of my reality came at me like wildfire. I had run out of Band-Aids, and the mirror of my father's regretful deathbed becoming my own became clear. What was there possibly left to distract me from the *real* issue? Nothing. I knew it was time to make the change to my life.

Don't get me wrong. Granite can be great. So are puppies, babies, fresh paint, and getaways, if you are with the right partner. Otherwise, you're only applying a Band-Aid to your damaged connection. If you *are* with the right person, granite (and all those other goodies) will indeed enhance your already fabulously close bond.

Note: If granite has not worked to "fix" your broken relationships, only you can decide if more distractions are worth the time and effort. If you do make the decision to stay or enter into a humdrum and unfulfilling relationship, you must be willing to live with the consequences of your decision. Being in the wrong relationship keeps you "unavailable" to find the right relationship, one that does not require slabs of granite to fix.

4

Become the accountant of your life spending.

Your Life Coin

Carl Sandburg wrote:

> *Time is the coin of your life. It is the only coin you have, and only you can determine how it will be spent. Be careful lest you let other people spend it for you.*

There has never been a more profound quotation when it comes to your love life. You have been given one—just one—precious life coin. I need you to spend it wisely! Imagine your life as a single coin, a special coin bestowed upon you by the universe the day you turn twenty-five years old. This one coin represents your entire life until the day you are on your deathbed. Each and every day of your life, you are spending a portion of your priceless life coin.

Unwise life-coin spending is the biggest love mistake we make as women. Don't fret if you've made some regretful purchases with your life coin. Trust me, it happens to most of us. The good news is prior inattentive spending of your life coin can still lead to the perfect purchase. However, from this point forward, I need you to be extremely cautious of how much of your coin you spend on a single purchase.

You may wonder why you are not given your life coin until you're twenty-five years old. Let me explain. Women in their early twenties are allowed to be a bit frivolous and carefree with their spending habits. The early twenties are all about experimenting with love. The early twenties are when I like to encourage women to find out what they like in a partner. And what they don't. It's a time to see what Dangs them and what doesn't. It's a time when a woman should access and focus on *her* life objectives and find her way through some obstacles of love.

However, if you are twenty-five years old or older, that is a different matter entirely and this chapter has your name written all over it.

The way you choose to spend your life coin is entirely up to you. For me, up until the time my father died, I had spent my life coin fairly well. I used a good portion of my coin to reach the most important goal in my life, which was to become a mother. I spent a fraction of my coin to obtain my education and a law degree. I spent a bit of my coin while I built my career as an attorney. Although I wasn't married to the love of my life during a majority of my spending, my first husband was instrumental in helping me to achieve some important life goals. For that, I am grateful, and it was a portion of my life coin well spent.

After my obvious life goals were met (marriage, children, education, home purchase) and after my father had died, I began to be much more cautious about my spending habits. Because I was already a mother of four, having children was no longer part of my life agenda. My motherhood box was closed with a big check mark on it. My new itinerary consisted of finding that mysterious feeling of love I had missed for twenty-five years.

With the majority of my life plan satisfied, I decided that the remaining portion of my coin could be spent on my quest for love and a fulfilled deathbed. Although my motherhood box had been checked off my list, I had to be realistic at the same time. I was now forty-four years old, and I had to think smart and spend smart. I had to be careful not to give away too many pennies to a prospective new partner who was not my Dang or with whom I had no future.

As you read *The Dang Factor*, I will share my personal life-coin stories and where my spending habits ultimately led me.

But first, I want you to ask yourself an important question: What are your life intentions? In other words, if you were to lie on your deathbed tomorrow, what would you regret not having accomplished? Is your plan to be married? Is becoming a mother of great importance to you? Is it important to experience deep love in your lifetime?

If the answer is yes to any or all of these last three questions, then you must be meticulous about how you spend your coin. Each brief purchase should be a learning lesson for your life. Each *brief purchase* should put you that much closer to reaching your life and deathbed aspirations.

What do I mean by a brief purchase? A brief life-coin purchase is one in which you are focused and mindful of your coin and the way it is being spent. How "brief" your purchase is will depend on your life design.

Let's say you're thirty-five years old and you meet Mr. Wonderful on Match.com. Sure, you can have fun and soak up the excitement of dating. You can even be exclusive with Mr. Wonderful for a *reasonable time*. So far, I have used the words "brief" and "reasonable." I hope you are starting to see a pattern here.

Not sticking to a reasonable period for dating is where many women misuse their coin. You are never too old to meet someone new or renew your current relationship. I was in my late forties when "The One" walked into my life. However, that being said, certain things, like our female eggs, do have an expiration date.

Your life coin is valuable at any time of your life. But it is an exceptionally rare coin to be polished during your childbearing years. If you remotely think for one minute that you want children and a family, and you're above the age of thirty, your coin is the most sacred of all.

Don't give away precious years to a partner who doesn't share the same dreams as you. I cannot tell you how many women I know who are now in their fifties and are not only without the man they wasted their coin on, but also without the children they so desperately wanted. That, my friends, is a tough pill to swallow.

So, what is reasonable and brief? If you are in your late twenties or older and you have been dating exclusively for a period of time, and you are not seriously discussing moving forward with plans to marry and make beautiful babies together, you need to think carefully about the way your coin is being spent.

You need to ask yourself this question: Are your daily spending habits furthering your life goals, or are you beginning to stagnate? You must stay focused and keep your eye on the prize as you plan your life. If your prize is marriage and babies, it is crucial to find the inner strength to plan accordingly and decide what a reasonable amount of time is for you to maintain the girlfriend or fiancée status.

We must cut the fluff and call it what it is. Dating is an audition; a tryout, an interview. Dating is a test, and you are being graded. During the dating process, men and women audition for each other for the ultimate role in the production of life: *marriage.*

Although dating is a mutual audition between prospective partners, there is one significant difference. When it comes to marriage, tying the knot, lifelong commitment, to have and to hold from this day forward, men hold all the cards. Yes, that's right. Your future is on *his* terms. If and when he is ready to pop the question, you are at *his* mercy. You are on *his* timeline. Men are the decision makers when it comes to *your* future. Wait! What?

Yes, from the beginning of time, it has been the man who makes the ultimate decision as to who will be his wife and, more importantly, when he will, if ever, pop the question. Now, don't get me wrong: I am all for tradition. In fact, I love the traditions of love. I adore and respect the historical gender roles. However, you must guide your ship on *your* timeline. Of course, your audition must go forward to find true love. However, you must be mindful of the length of *your* interview. That is the power *you* hold.

I caution you not to participate in a typical situation I like to call the "I will continue to date her and get unlimited sex and wait to see if someone better comes along whom I will actually commit to" syndrome. Don't allow years of your coin to be spent on a one-sided romance. What I *do* want you to do is create a situation in which, after a *reasonable* amount of time, your man cannot wait to make you his bride and shout his commitment from the highest mountain. What I want for you is good love!

A common relationship blunder women make is to adopt the "If I just give him a bit more time, he will come around" mentality. The question you must ask is, do you have enough time on your coin to give away? Remember, every day you stay with a partner who ultimately does not commit to marriage and family will amount to one more day that you are not available to seek love and start the life you desire.

Quite often the issue of commitment is not the idea of marriage, per se. The hesitation is most likely based on the perception of marriage *with* a particular partner. This may hold true for you or someone you know. How many people do you know whose former partner did not want marriage or children and then went on to marry and have children with a new partner?

Be aware of the passing days, months, and years of your life. If you are content to try out for years for the role of wife or mother, you must be prepared for the consequences if you do not get the starring role. The consequence, of course, is that you do not get married to your current partner and, perhaps, you do not achieve your dream of motherhood. Both age and the passage of time will have an effect on your visions and desires.

If your man wants to be married to *you*, he will. He will want to be married sooner rather than later. Why? Quite simply, he does not want to risk losing the woman of his dreams.

If, after a reasonable amount of time, no answer *is* your answer, it may be time to move forward and find yourself a partner who truly wants to commit to every inch of you. *Both* feet of *both* partners need to be in the relationship and dedicated to a future together. A partner with just one foot in leaves one foot *out*. That is not the kind of partnership I want you in.

W.W.Y.T.? (Why Waste Your Time?)

These are all true scenarios from women I interviewed for *The Dang Factor.* These scenarios might indicate you could be wasting too many pennies on a current or future partner:

1. You definitely want children, and he's had a vasectomy.
2. He lives in Los Angeles, and you live in Boston. Neither of you is willing to relocate to the opposite coast.
3. You have three children, and he has made it clear he wants a future wife who has no children.
4. He is married, separated, or currently semi-attached to his wife or ex-girlfriend.
5. His Facebook profile says "Married" or "In a Relationship." *(And he does not mean with you.)*
6. Pictures of his ex are all over his social media, and he will not remove them. (*I would call this an attachment issue, to his ex.*)
7. He told you he does not want to get married. Ever.
8. You went on a trip with him to Australia where you gave him a marriage ultimatum after dating for five years. Three years later, you are still not married to him. *(You have now spent eight years of your life on this unequivocally non-committing man.)*

9. He is a professional snowboarder who is moving to Alaska, and he does not touch alcohol. You hate the cold, despise snow, love Chardonnay, and refuse to move to Alaska. *(Need I say more?)*

As you date, I need you to think about where you are in life. If you're at a point in your life plan where you can afford to spend your coin on three to five years of dating one person, then, by all means, do it.

My goal is to awaken the financial accountant within you and assess our debits used on love. I would like for you to have a life plan as you navigate the waters of dating and relationships. Just as you have a household-spending budget you live by each month, so too must you have a life budget as you spend each penny of your gifted coin.

The Dress

It is helpful to think of your current, past, or future partner as a dress. You know, the kind of dress you put on to go to a special event. When you first bought the dress, it fit you well. It was flattering to your figure, and you felt wonderful when you wore that dress.

However, after some time, the dress did not fit you quite as well. In fact, every time you put the dress on, you did not like what you saw in the mirror. Your favorite dress started to have a different feel to it. So, you shortened the dress, you let the seams out, you took the seams in, you let the hem down, and you took the hem up. No matter what you did to try to fix the dress, it just did not fit the same way it used to.

I want you to begin to recognize when your partner (like your dress) may no longer be a good fit for you. Do not get comfortably settled into a relationship rut with a dress that clearly does not fit you and your life. It could be time to donate the dress (aka your ill-fitting partner) to Goodwill and buy a new, better-fitting dress that will require very limited alterations.

After my father died, I had to make a choice regarding the ill-fitting dress I had been wearing for a quarter of a century. For me, my decision to leave my marriage and search for a better fitting dress was life changing. I stepped into the unknown and let my courage outdo my fear. I found peace with being alone or possibly never finding my new dress if that was the outcome of my search for real love. We must not let the fear of being alone paralyze us from making changes to our lives. The alternative of no change will most certainly rob us of all future possibilities.

Your Life Coin and Counseling

As a divorce attorney and life advisor, I'm often asked about relationship counseling and the success it may have in a floundering relationship. In other words, is relationship or marriage counseling a wise use of your life coin? My answer: It depends.

For me, all the counseling in the world would not have fixed my prior marriage. Why? Simple. He was not my Dang. He was never my Dang, and without that crucial element, counseling would have been a waste of time. A counselor or therapist cannot create a Dang. The Dang you feel for someone is black and white. There is no gray area of Dang.

With that being said, I do believe occasional counseling can help to keep an otherwise good relationship on track; To fine-tune it, if you will. Again, be cautious of the number of pennies you spend on your tune-ups. If your entire relationship is so far off track with issues such as habitual cheating or polar opposite values and goals, it may be time to think about less counseling and, instead, a trip to Nordstrom to buy a better-fitting dress.

Terri is an excellent example of over counseling and excessive spending of her coin. Terri has been in a non-married relationship with Greg for fifteen years. Terri has spent years trying to make her dress fit. Terri and Greg have lived together and then lived apart. They became engaged and then unengaged. They have broken up and reconciled more than twenty times.

Their families dislike each other, and it changes weekly as to whether Terri and Greg can stand each other. They have been in couples counseling for more than ten years. Terri is no closer to getting married to Greg (or anyone else for that matter) than when the relationship started fifteen years ago. As Terri approaches her sixtieth birthday, I can't help but be saddened by the love lost and negative energy both Terri and Greg have expended on their uncommitted union.

I recently had a conversation about *The Dang Factor* with a friend who is a marriage therapist. She makes her living trying to keep couples together. It is of little importance to my friend if the couple is a good match or not. My friend does not care if the couple have long outgrown each other. It does not matter to my counselor friend if either partner feels a morsel of love for the other.

In my friend's practice, she promotes division of labor regarding household chores as a means of making the troubled relationship work. My friend believes that if she divides up the housework and child duties between the two partners, the marriage will be saved. My friend believes that if she counsels one partner to be more thoughtful and the other partner to be less sensitive, the relationship will become golden. In my opinion (and experience), that is simply not true. If the underlying *Dang* is missing, I don't care how many dishes one partner gets told to wash. A clean house does not make a Dang.

Unlike marriage therapists and counselors, who are in the business of trying to keep couples together (regardless of whether they are a good match), I am in the business of helping you make positive life choices that will lead to good love. I am not here to encourage your breakup. Instead, my mission is to promote your happiness and introduce you to the tingle of Dang I want you to feel for your partner.

Overall, I have no issue with relationship counseling. The key, of course, is that you *want* your relationship to rebuild and flourish.

For counseling to be beneficial, the crucial element that must be present in the relationship is a *mutual* desire to resurrect your bond. You can get counseling and therapy until pigs fly, but unless there is some morsel of mutual Dang between you both, counseling is not likely to be useful.

I have personally lived this issue, and trust me when I tell you no amount of counseling could have turned my ex-husband into my desired partner. Many counselors and therapists often have not personally experienced what a Dang feels like. It is not learned from a textbook or by getting your PhD. It is not found in therapy psychobabble. There is no "science" to relationships, as some self-proclaimed experts want you to believe. The Dang phenomenon is learned from real-life relationships and is something I want *you* to experience during your lifetime.

Remember, my therapist friend's attempt to fix a Dang-less marriage by trying to delegate housework is how she makes a living. If she were to tell you there was no hope of making your relationship work and that it was time to move on, my friend would not get paid and would have no income. Take the idea of marriage counseling for what it is worth. If he is your Dang, simple fix-its such as housework may resolve the issue. If he *is not* your Dang, he could vacuum until eternity and he will still never achieve the requisite Dang status.

How you choose to spend your coin will ultimately determine the direction of your life. The most wonderful thing is that *you* get to decide what kind of shopping spree to take your life on.

As the years of our lives tick forward, we must understand we get just one shot at this life of ours. No do-overs. No go-backs. No more chances. I have friends who have not changed a single thing about their lives in thirty years. They have lived in the same house. They have kept the same routine. They have coasted through the same life without any change, challenge, adventure, or self-improvement. They have complained about their spouses for years, and they *still* complain about them some thirty years later.

The intention of *The Dang Factor* is to promote your happiness and empower you to change the way you seek and experience love. It is about your dreams. It is about your goals in life and love and the best way to achieve them. You alone hold the key to a fulfilled and delightfully love-soaked life.

You know what breaks my heart? Knowing people I care about will not feel the adoring love they so deserve. It breaks my heart to know people I care about will be unnecessarily single or terribly unsatisfied and lonely in their relationship for the rest of their lives. And most profoundly, I know some people I love will never experience the beauty of motherhood because they gave their life coin away to some jerk.

I want you to take charge of your spending and steer your own ship into your personal harbor of happiness.

5

*For every love there is a category.
But not every category has love.*

Relationship Status Check-In

It's time for your relationship status check-in. Let's get started!

Okay, so maybe you are single and ready to meet the love of your life. Or possibly you are thinking about venturing out into the dating world to jump-start your love life. Maybe your marriage did not work out the way you had hoped.

Possibly your relationship is headed in a downhill direction, and you want to revive it. Maybe your Dang became your Dud. Maybe your Dud was never your Dang.

Perhaps your boyfriend never made that marriage commitment to you. Maybe your partner cheated. Maybe he found someone else. Maybe you finally realized your family and friends were right: He was a jerk. Maybe now you understand that you have not been prudently spending your coin. Maybe you have realized this is *your* life, and there will be no do-overs.

As women, we tend to tolerate (or ignore) unfulfilling and unhealthy relationships for many years. We are inclined to continue each day and hope something will click to somehow make the relationship come to life. As we wait for the magic to happen, we fill our lives with one distraction after the next until *hopefully*, one day, something will happen that will propel us to make a big life change.

I say "hopefully" because it is that one day or moment in time that will thrust you forward in life. And then, suddenly, boom! We check out. Every ounce of feeling and emotion we ever had for that person has now vanished.

What's incredible about women is that, once we check out, there is little hope of ever checking back in. Our emotions and feelings simply do not work that way. Men, sure, they can check in and out of a relationship depending on their moods, sexual desires, and convenience factors. We women? Well, our brains and bodies just don't work like that.

Once we have exhausted every conceivable way to fix it, many women do eventually come to realize the granite (or anything

3. You Need to Fix Your Current Relationship or You *May* Be Single
4. I Found My Dang, and We Are Loving Life Together!

1. Single

If your current status is single, that's awesome. Why? Because I know somewhere along your life path, you made a decision (or a decision was made *for* you) that your past relationship was not the Dang love you deserve. If your past relationship had indeed been your true mutual Dang, quite frankly, you would not be single.

Committed love *must be mutual*, meaning you need to lust for your partner just as much as he lusts for you and vice versa. If you previously thought you met "The One" and he did not move mountains to make a commitment to your future together, it is safe to say that the Dang Factor was missing for one or both of you. Devoted couples do not break up.

Your current single status is the perfect starting point as you navigate your way through *The Dang Factor* and soak up your path to love. I am so excited for your journey!

2. Should Be Single

We have all seen it. How many times have you gone to a restaurant and watched a couple not speak a word to one another? They stay married for the sake of being married and robotically go through the daily motions of life. These couples have ab olutely nothing in common and most likely have not touch l each other in years. No affection. No emotion. No war h between them.

T may have been in love at one time, or maybe they weren't. fact is that they are no longer in mutual love. These couples y have grown tired of each other or have simply taken two different directions in life. It happens, and you know what? It's okay.

What does a "should be single" state mean? It means that instead of using the limited time you have on this earth to seek and absorb good love, you have made the choice to stay put in a convenient or brotherly love. When love is void in your life, you may be better off single, so your journey to real love can truly begin.

A "should be single" status can come about from many things. Maybe you were madly in love at one time, but something changed along the way. You may have grown and blossomed as a person, and he did not. Maybe you ultimately sought two different paths in life. Possibly one or both of you just outgrew each other. Or maybe you should be single because, well, frankly, you are in a relationship with an ass and have finally realized you will never change him or the crappy relationship you are in.

Chat Room Check-In

To demonstrate what "should be single" means, I am going to share some real-life posts by women interviewed for T*he Dang*

Factor. I wish I could say these are unique statements, but they follow a pattern found among the more than two thousand women I interviewed. Of course, the names have been changed, but the sentiments resonate just the same. How does your current or past relationship measure up in the "should be single" category?

> Sandy: *Is it bad that the only possible way I can have sex with my husband is if I am drunk? I have no attraction to him at all. I filed for divorce once, but when I found out how little money I would get for support, I decided to stick it out forever. I stock up on vodka at Costco and deal with it.*

> Elizabeth: *I am wishing my period on me. My husband is coming home after a long trip, and the thought of sex with him is making me cringe!*

> Emily: *I'm reading about vow renewals on the Internet and wishing I had someone I wanted to renew vows with. I mean nothing to my husband. He spends every minute he has playing golf. I'm so resentful that I do all of the dirty work at home, cleaning our entire home with a bad neck and back, when he does nothing to help. We recently had our twelfth wedding anniversary, and he didn't even acknowledge it. Nothing. Not even a card. I'm crying a lot on the inside and outside. If we divorced, he'd be so happy. Do we, as women, just have to come to grips that we will always be miserable? I'm tired and worn down. He hasn't told me he loves me in over three years.*

Jessica: *I'm miserable in my marriage. I'm tired, and Cinderella wants to go to the ball. I'm not young and not old but am in sort of a mid-life crisis pondering how I want to spend the rest of my life. The one thing I know for sure is I do not want to spend the rest of my life with him.*

Katie: *My mother tells me to get my own life. She says, "Do you think you are the only woman who has felt miserable in her marriage? You will not change him, and men who are rotten do not change."*

Terri: *When we added a child to our marriage, it made me realize it's more about him. When he is home, he's resting or on his computer. I never feel like a family. I think about when I am an empty nester if I will have any emotions left for him. I feel absolutely nothing for him. I take care of my son and move forward. I work full-time on purpose so that we see very little of each other. He chooses to work weekends when I am home. I have expressed my frustration to him, but he doesn't listen. I have no feeling left in my body.*

Marsha: *Every morning, I wake up and go exercise. He asks for the remote control to watch sports recaps like clockwork on the sports channel. I'm over it. I swear if a TV had a vagina most men would be set for life. We have not had sex in over two years. I wish he would just go away.*

Kristen: *I just got the silent treatment for eight days while he's on a work trip because I told him before he left that I do not feel "good enough" for him. He, of course, spun it around and now he's playing the victim card. We live in awkward silence on a daily basis. I wish his work trips would last for years at a time. Fuck My Life.*

Marie: *Being married to my man is bullshit. I mean, it was fun at the beginning, but the quality of man I married compares equally to the dog poop in the backyard. Personally, I cannot stand him.*

Jennifer: *Is it bad that every time my husband comes home from work I am praying that I get the flu, so I don't have to have sex with him?*

Kristen: *I would just like you all to know you are not the only women who are in bullshit relationships. I literally begged my husband in a six-page letter to be nice to me, to say a kind word here and there, basically treat me like a human being. I'm sick of not being good enough in about a million different ways. He told me the reason he isn't nice is that I'm overweight and he can't live with it. He has refused to have sex with me for the past three years. Yeah, I'm living the dream here, ladies!*

Kellie: *Anyone track your husband's phone when he heads home from work? I do, and I dread it. It's going to be a complete shit show when he comes home today. Three days ago, he told me, "I'm not happy." We just went through this literally three months ago. "The house is never clean enough. You are overweight and the fattest out of all of your friends. Don't you even care what you look like? I have no attraction to you at all," he says. When do I just say fuck it, give up, and call him on his bluff? Each time he does this, it hurts less and less.*

Diana's Story—Begging to Be Desired

One of the most disturbing stories I received came from Diana. Some of the reactions from other women in the forum were equally troubling. It is *not okay* to be the subject of not being wanted, adored, and desired by your partner. Do you really want to have to try to convince your partner you're worthy of his sexual desires? Conversely, do you really want to be in a relationship where you have absolutely no desire for your partner?

I share Diana's story because I know she's not the only woman out there who needs to take back her life. I share it because I want you to feel mutual adoration with your partner. Please heed this message before you are ninety years old and it's too damn late to go backward and walk away from or correct a situation such as Diana's. I want to guide you to live your life with a partner who cannot wait to spend time with you and touch every inch of you. I want you to begin to love *you* first and to never spend a day with a partner who does not crave and adore you. My response follows each post (in parentheses).

> Diana: *I bought a sexy outfit to wear when I greeted my husband at the door when he came home from work today. He came in the door, looked at me, and said, "I am not feeling well." He went straight to the couch, watched TV for three hours, and went to bed. Today, I asked him if he desires me at all, and he said he doesn't think that way. I asked him if I should work to change my body, and he said to do whatever makes me happy. I asked him if I turn him on at all. He answered, "I don't know. I don't think that way. Can you just leave me alone? I have no interest in anything with you." I cannot believe this is my life.*

It makes me so sad.

Erin: *Is it because he's sick?*

Diana: *No, he is not sick. Today, he told me again that he doesn't see me that way. It crushes me. I love him and would do anything for him. Obviously, I don't do anything for him. It makes me sad. But I'll keep trying! (Diana, an integral part of being someone's Dang is having the strength and self-worth to settle for nothing less than being the object of your partner's desires.)*

Vanessa: *Maybe he is going through a mid-life change. Have you had his testosterone levels checked?*

Diana: *No, he's been this way for ten years. It has nothing to do with him being sick or any kind of low levels. He flat out told me he is not attracted to me. I guess I just don't do it for him and he has refused to talk to me about it. (Diana, you are much too fabulous to beg your man to want you!)*

Trish: *I had my guy checked too. He has no interest in me either. I had hoped it was low, but it was perfectly normal.*

Diana: *Never say die, and I am never giving up. (Diana, please be aware of the precious pennies you are going to spend trying to persuade your husband to want to touch you.)*

Cara: *Similar circumstances in my home. My husband told me the same thing.*

Bonnie: *Oh, man. That has to hurt! Maybe you caught him off guard.*

Susan: *Do not badger or pester him—believe me, I speak from experience—it will only drive him away. (If you tell your husband you want to be loved, adored, and desired by him and it drives him away, it may be time for a new dress.)*

Diana: *No, I didn't throw him off guard. He's been telling me the same thing for ten years. It's no big deal. I have vented. I'm good now. (Diana, it is a big deal because you deserve mutual love.)*

Dee: *He will come around. (It has been ten years. How long do we think Diana should wait to be desired by her husband?)*

Kristen: *Diana, for you to say for the last ten years he has been this way and follow it up with, "I've vented, I'm better now" is the saddest thing I have ever heard. I think you need to look a little deeper and talk to someone. You should not have to settle for a complete lack of love. If you love someone, it must be reciprocated. Trust me when I tell you I have been in your situation, and I had to let it go. I am not saying for you to do the same, but you have to love yourself and have enough respect for yourself to get the same back from your partner. (Kristen, you're right. Diana's love needs to be equally reciprocated, or it really is not love at all.)*

3. You Need to Fix Your Current Relationship or You May Be Single

This status of your life is an entirely different can of worms than the two relationship situations we have already discussed. In the "you need to fix your current relationship" status, there is still an underlying *mutual* Dang left between you and your partner. With a fragment of Dang still felt by both of you, your relationship may just require a bit of polishing to reboot and get back on track. I cannot stress enough the importance of putting in the effort to save your relationship, if and *only if*, you *both* have some crumb of Dang left in you. To fix and revive your once-felt attraction and devotion, both partners must feel (and want) some potential hope for love revival.

So how do you know if your relationship still has some underlying and mutual Dang left in it? Simple. Take the "Dang Test."

Dang Test Question 1: If, after you had split up, you were to see your ex walk, hand in hand, into a restaurant with another woman, how would you feel?

Before you answer that question, take note: the first "Dang Test" rule explicitly states that you cannot have it both ways. In other words, can't say you aren't attracted to or interested in being with your partner and at the same time tell me seeing him with another woman would turn you into a jealous jellyfish. Remember, either you Dang or you don't. Even a fragment of Dang is still a Dang.

For me, the thought of my ex-husband with another woman didn't bother me in the slightest. I felt total indifference at the thought of him with another woman. I couldn't have cared less. By the time I ended our marriage, I was so far checked out that any jealous emotions were long gone. I did not feel a crumb of sexual attraction to him. In fact, I wanted him to find love and move forward with his life so he, too, could experience what good love is.

Dang Test Question 2: How do you feel when your partner touches you?

If you do not enjoy being touched by your partner, it could be a sign that your Dang has died or is temporarily out of order. Intimate touch between your partner and you is the one thing that sets your relationship apart from that of a guy friend. It's that shared sexual intimacy that marks your relationship as different from what you share with coworkers, friends, and neighbors. Sex, kissing, hugging, and holding hands are the components that classify you both as a "couple." Sexual touches are the things you *do not* do with your friends, neighbors, and coworkers (at least I hope you don't) and are reserved specifically for your partner. If you are not touching, well then, you are simply living as roommates.

In my case, although my ex-husband was a nice guy, I had no desire to be touched by him. I did not want to kiss him, be held by him, or, heaven forbid, have sex with him. I avoided touching at all costs and made up excuses to avoid intimacy. Looking back, I now realize there was nothing "wrong" with me for not wanting sex; it was quite simply that I was not married to my Dang.

Once you determine if there *is* an aspect of Dang in your relationship, how do you go about pulling your relationship out of the fix-it stage? Easy. You put in the effort. You rearrange your priorities so your partner comes first (before your friends, the kids, or the dog), like when you were dating.

You will need to step outside of *you* and look in to find the current state of your relationship. If there is still some Dang and you are just going through a rough patch or have become disconnected as a couple, it is not necessary to end the marriage. If you passed my two-pronged "Dang Test," there is hope for love resurrection, and it is time to get serious about bringing good love back into your life.

4. I Found My Dang, and We Are Loving Life Together

This last status speaks for itself. The key word in this status of your life is "together." I cannot emphasize the need for mutual desire enough. Not a Diana, one-sided kind of love, but instead a love and affection for each other that radiates off both of you.

Evaluate Your Status

Now that you have read and absorbed the four different relationship status categories, I hope you will be able to step back and look objectively in at your status to evaluate which category you fall (or should fall) into.

If your current life situation is "single," that is fantastic, and I hope you will spend your coin wisely on your journey to love.

If you conclude you fall into the "should be single" status, I applaud you for coming to the realization that you deserve to be mutually desired, adored, and loved by your partner.

I will use Diana as the best example of a "should be single" status. In Diana's case, all emotional and physical bonds have long been broken, and all that has remained of the "marriage" is their legal tie to each other. Although Diana has much love for her husband, it is clear her husband has no meaningful love left for Diana.

For the past ten years, Diana's husband has been emotionally and physically checked out of their marriage. A lopsided love or a love felt by only one partner is no love at all. I don't want you to spend your life coin trying to convince someone how incredibly awesome you are. I know it, you should know it, and the future love of your life will definitely know it.

If your current status reflects a "you need to fix your current relationship" state of existence, I must caution you. If you are presently in a relationship and you are considering ending it for whatever reason, I want you to think long (but not too long) and hard about your decision. If you still feel *some* Dang (however slight) for your partner, move cautiously in your decision to end the relationship. If an indiscretion or isolated event has led to your decision to walk away, I caution you to let your emotions settle before making any move toward a final breakup.

Do not listen to your friends or family regarding your decision to end a relationship. *You* are the one who will live with the consequences of your decision. Only *you* can evaluate the part each of you has played in the current status of your relationship.

An example of a "you need to fix your current relationship or you may be single" status are my friends Darla and Peter. Darla and Peter have been married for ten years. They have two small children. Darla is a stay-at-home mom. Peter is a lawyer. Both Darla and Peter are kind and wonderful people.

After ten years, Darla started to feel antsy in her marriage and questioned whether someone better and more exciting was out there. Peter, on the other hand, was completely smitten and devoted to Darla. When she shared this with me, I asked her one question: When Peter walks into the room, do you feel *any* Dang for him? Her answer: "Yes."

That was the answer I needed to hear. With that, my conversation with Darla focused on reminding her how lucky she was to feel that sweet morsel of attraction for her husband. Remember, a morsel of Dang is still a Dang. I also made it clear that if she were to release Peter into the dating pool, he *would* have women lined up to date and marry him. She needed to be prepared for that. That detail is something Darla had never thought about.

Darla realized she had become complacent about making Peter and their marriage a priority. Darla had allowed the kids, the soccer games, the gymnastics classes, and a hectic life to overshadow the great marriage they once had. Darla set out to regain the closeness she and Peter once shared.

In my friend Cindy's case, both she and her husband felt a great attraction for each other. Over the years, however, Cindy's draw to her husband has diminished. The reason Cindy's attraction waned is that she does not think her husband is driven in his career and is not contributing to the household expenses. Cindy is fixing it by encouraging and guiding her man on a new career path. Even better, her man is responsive and has returned to school in pursuit of a more satisfying and lucrative career. Cindy pinpointed the missing link in her marriage and is on her way back to a stronger love with her husband.

On the flip side, I know several women who do nothing but analyze their marriages ad nauseam. Be careful not to miss out on the sheer enjoyment of what you *have* in your relationship because you are so consumed with what you *don't have.*

Here is an example of an over-analytical wife who could very well analyze her marriage straight to a divorce:

> Katie: *My husband and I are going through a rough patch in our marriage. I'm at a point where I'm not sure what to do. My struggle is that our love languages don't match up and it's wearing me down. I'm physical touch and affirmation and he is quality time and acts of service. I'm hesitant to have kids because of these struggles and differences, yet my husband looks past them because he desperately wants kids. When I share my*

concerns, instead of trying to change, he tells me I am the love of his life and to stop analyzing our love. (Katie, your husband is right. Stop analyzing. I know a ton of women who would love quality time and acts of service. As long as he is servicing you and giving you quality time, you are one lucky girl.)

If one or both of you choose not to put effort into the revitalization of your once fun and sexy marriage, you could end up divorced. You both need to be prepared for this and the realization that you could lose an otherwise incredible love when all that was needed was a bit of polishing and effort.

They are the hunters of our hearts and the occasional insanity of our souls.

The (Cave) Men

Most of the time, men are delightfully simple and incredibly easy creatures to understand and love. With a touch of female guidance, men are fairly basic beings. Although men may seem complex, they really are quite uncomplicated and predictable. My research for this chapter (and *The Dang Factor*) included interviews with more than two thousand men who gave me the straight scoop directly from the source.

During my twenty-year career as a divorce attorney, I interviewed thousands of men from every walk of life. I questioned plumbers, truck drivers, store clerks, doctors, lawyers, and pilots. I spoke to _e middle class, the rich, and the poor. I spoke to younger men and older men. When I asked what they needed in a strong and committed relationship, their answers never varied. Each one said the same five things over and over.

So, here is the very short list that I refer to as the "Fab Five":

1. Good Sex
2. Good Food and Drink
3. Long Live the Dang Factor
4. Value Your Partner
5. Let Him Be the (Cave) Man He Was Born to Be

That's it. Truly. It's shockingly simple. Let's dive into the first of the Fab Five.

(Note: The Fab Five will be useful to you only if you are in a relationship with mutual *love. Without a crumb of Dang, this list of five will have little value. However, keep it handy for future reference because you never know when love will surprise the hell out of you.)*

Fab Five #1: Good Sex

This is by far the number one priority for a man in a relationship. Men need it. Men crave it. Men cannot live without it. If you are with a partner you dig, you will need and crave sex too. Yes, it's true. With the right partner, you will desire sex as much as or more than he does. If you are not with the right guy, chances are you have virtually no sex drive and probably try like hell to avoid intimacy. I say that because that is exactly what I did for twenty-five years during my first marriage.

Trust me when I tell you this: Sex with the proper partner is the most incredible feeling on earth. As women, we *need* to be with our Dang to want sex. I truly thought I had no sex drive during my first marriage. I had no interest in sex. I came up with every excuse in the world to avoid sex. On a scale of one to ten, my sex drive for all of those precious years of my life was a big fat zero.

At one point, I saw a doctor about "my problem," because I assumed there must be something physically wrong with me. I had multiple blood tests done to make sure my hormone levels were normal and to find out what was "wrong." My test results revealed a normal, healthy female with perfectly balanced hormone levels.

So what the heck was going on? One answer: I was not married to the right person. My ex-husband was a kind man. He was funny, thoughtful, sweet, and caring. But he was not my Dang.

Four years following my divorce, I met my current husband. Just let me say one thing loud and clear: *What a difference a Dang makes!* I was blown away by how my body, mind, and soul craved sexual intimacy. His smile, his smell, a touch on the small of my back, a slight kiss on my neck . . . well, the doctors were right; my hormone levels were perfectly primed and ready—for the right guy. I never knew my body had any sexual feelings until they came alive with the right partner.

Still, more than ten years later, every fiber of my being craves him. I know, it sounds crazy, but it's true. The total and complete wanting of your partner is the most mind-blowing and soul-fulfilling feeling imaginable. It is something every woman deserves to experience in her lifetime.

For those of you who are or have been in detached and lonely relationships, imagine you begin to date a man whom you think is quite attractive. What is on your mind as you sit across the table from him while you sip your wine? *Sex!* Why? Because you have come alive with feelings of arousal, desire, yearning, and excitement. *Those* are the sensations and emotions we need to feel in our own present-day lives. Oh, and trust me, you do have a sex drive. Chances are your sex drive has simply gone into remission and may simply need a jump-start.

Many of the men I spoke with complained about sex being held against them. There is no bigger tension builder between couples than when sex has come to a screeching halt or is a rare occurrence. Think back to when you were dating and the pattern of intimacy. Sex was likely a high priority during your dating years. Either partner's pleading for sex as the years go forward is demeaning and damaging to your union.

I am in no way proposing that you *need* to have mind-blowing sex with your partner on a daily basis. If that works for you, more power to you. The frequency of sex is whatever works for you, as a couple. Both partners need to be *reasonably* satisfied. I repeat, reasonably satisfied. I am not suggesting extremes here.

Fab Five #2: Good Food and Drink

Pretty basic, right? Combine Fab Five #1 and #2, and your guy is pretty much putty in your hands. I am not proposing you aim for Martha Stewart perfection, but a nice meal, some homemade goodies, and a cold beer make for a very satisfied man. The mere thought of buying the special cheese he likes or learning to make that one Italian dessert he loves means more to him than you would think. These small gestures, the thoughtfulness as to what he likes to eat and drink, make him feel loved and appreciated. It's simple, but as the saying goes, "The way to a man's heart is through his stomach." Bon appétit!

Fab Five #3: Long Live the Dang Factor

All relationships begin with some element of dating. Do you remember when you were dating and each of you put effort into planning and getting ready for your date? A slice of that same effort should exist and stay present as the years go on.

Sure, we all get more comfortable in our relationships. It is amazing to be with someone with whom you can be yourself and just relax. That is one of the many perks of a long-term relationship. But we need to be careful lest we take comfort too far. Ease and familiarity should not replace energy from both of you to maintain the once-ignited spark.

Too much comfort in a relationship is a dangerous and risky ingredient to add to the batter of love. Getting too comfortable in marriage is when problems begin to mount. When effort to maintain the marital connection is replaced by comfort and indifference, a relationship can slowly start to crumble. Taking one's partner for granted is the biggest complaint I received about fraying marriages.

I get it. We get married, and we get contented. Contentment is a good thing to an extent. I mean, who doesn't love a comfy pair of sweats on a cold winter's day? On my bad hair days (of which I have many), a top bun is my go-to hairstyle. However, although comfort in a relationship is blissful, comfort should not replace effort from either partner. Contentment should not replace nurture. Coziness should not replace sweet gestures. And, more importantly, comfort should not replace sex and the incredible power of touch with your partner.

It is important that both of you continue to make the effort to at least semi-resemble (emotionally, spiritually, and physically) the person each partner was dating and ultimately married. Once married, it is essential to maintain a semblance of the individual each of you fell in love with. As humans, we need to feel wanted, loved, and appreciated, especially by our partner. During the dating process, we demonstrate our love and appreciation for our partner through loving gestures, outward affection, thoughtful planning, and lots of touching.

I am not suggesting we keep the momentum of the courting process going for the entirety of the marriage. Obviously, we do reach a certain plateau of comfort and security in a long-term relationship. What I *am* suggesting is continued energy and thought from *each partner* to keep the love light burning. The sweet compliments and gestures during the glorious days of dating should not fall prey to the beast of comfort love.

Getting too comfortable in your marriage and losing the desire to put in the effort is a danger zone I do not want either of you to enter. You and your partner are the nucleus of the family. When you two are connected and close, everything else will fall into place. When partners fall into a mundane and monotonous routine, it sends the marriage into a freefall.

The question most asked of me by the thousands of men and women I interviewed for *The Dang Factor*: "Where did that person I married disappear to? Where is the person I was dating? You know, the fun-loving, adventurous, confident, sex-loving, thoughtful, and upbeat person I married." It is vital that the person we date and ultimately marry stays present throughout the relationship.

It is hard work to keep a relationship healthy. Every marriage is going to have its ups and downs. The kids are going to make us crazy. Our jobs are going to drive us nuts. Our partner is going to grate on our last nerve. We are going to be beat-ass tired. The point I am making here is that, in spite of all the crap life hands us, we need to stay aware not to enter a comfort zone that replaces the effort of love.

Fab Five #4: Value Your Partner

Men are fairly simple creatures. A bit of recognition and appreciation goes a long way. I cannot emphasize enough the response you will get if you recognize and thank him for what he is doing *right* in the relationship versus bringing up all the things he is doing *wrong*.

During my interviews, one thing the men kept coming back to was their perception of the male role in the modern day relationship. I must agree with their notion that the male position has become significantly diminished over time. Men feel this change in their role as the patriarch of the family, and the change has affected them.

I am not by any means suggesting we go back to the 1950s, when the family roles were more clearly defined. However, an acknowledgment of his position as being equal in value to your position is monumental to his self-esteem. This is an area where our men do get a tad complex. Their need for our reassurance and approval is vital to their self-confidence.

Step outside and look *in* at each of your roles in the relationship. Do you think of him as an equal and valued partner? A good method I like to use is the "Listen In" test when I speak to my husband. It has been a great tool as I step outside of *me* and listen *in* to my tone of voice when I talk to him. To "listen in," simply take a breath and listen from the outside in, to your voice, your mannerisms, and your message, as if you were eavesdropping on another couple.

The words "You are such an ass, and you never do anything around the house" will not make him want to jump up and take out the trash any more than his saying "You are a slob" would make you want to be organized and motivated. It is our tone of voice that is so compelling to the way we interpret the words spoken. The old saying "It's not what you say but how you say it" is true. Imagine a stranger walking by and hearing either of you talk to the other. What do you think your conversation would sound like? For me personally, I was surprised by the way I sounded at times!

I can hear some of you saying, "Well, he doesn't show me he appreciates me, either." That may be true. But we need to start somewhere. It is not a competition between the two of you. Initially, someone has to be the leader of niceness in your relationship, and I would like it to be you. I want you to take the lead. Even if you do not believe it, say it. If he hears praise or thanks often enough, you may be surprised by what happens. I have found that magical things happen when I give more praise and appreciation and a lot less nagging. Telling your partner how much you appreciate and value him will soon become a sort of self-fulfilling prophecy.

Fab Five #5: Let Him Be the (Cave) Man He Was Born to Be

Men want to lead and protect. Men want to feel like men and act as the patriarch of the family. Men want to be instrumental in family decisions. Simply put, men want to be heard and want their opinion to have some value.

Trust me, it took every inch of my being to stop being a control freak. With great restraint, I learned to let him make some decisions for the family and stop stressing about the "wrong" decision he might make. I learned to let him make assessments, right or wrong, and allow the two of us to live with the result without routinely throwing the decision back at him.

Help him to find comfort in being the (cave) man. Many men have taken a back seat to their male role, and the men made their reason clear to me: Men would rather take a step back than be griped at by their women. Maybe the restaurant he surprised you with for dinner was not so great. What's important is that *he* picked it. Maybe that's not how you would have organized the cupboard or packed the dishwasher or dressed your toddler. The fact is, he did the chore, and it's okay for him to do it his way. The more we criticize and complain, the less inclined he'll be to pitch in the next time.

Just as the original caveman took pride in foraging for food, give him the opportunity to make decisions without over criticizing. Our partners should not feel afraid of our reaction if, heaven forbid, he comes home with the wrong type of cereal from the grocery store. Corn puffs vs. corn flakes? Who cares? Hey, at least he went to the store! Even if I do not agree with it, or he made what I consider to be a poor decision, I have learned if I bite my tongue, it will make a positive impact in our relationship.

If you are single and dating, I will add the following to the Fab Five list: Do not chase him. I am not saying to play games. What I am saying is simply respect the gender roles. By all means, you can make the first move. That is perfectly fine. In fact, I encourage it. However, once he has your contact information, and you have made your interest known, let him do the pursuing.

In true Caveman fashion, let him date you. Let him court you. If he wants to see you, he has your number. Do not chase him down. If he wants to see you, talk to you, or plan a date with you, he will. It was unanimous in my male interviews: If he is not pursuing you, he is not interested.

When my husband was pursuing me, I was astounded by the number of women who continued to chase him. Jenny, a woman he had gone on a few dates with, was persistent in her pursuit of him. Jenny would send multiple text messages and emails asking when she could see him next and making herself *very* available. Jenny, he has your number. Trust me, if it's not ringing, he is not interested. If a man wants to contact you, he will. Otherwise, no answer is your answer.

Do not take the Fab Five elements out of context. When I am referring to the (cave) man, I am referencing everyday living. I am not referring to major purchases or obvious decisions that partners make together, for example, budgeting, spending on large purchases, home and car purchases, where to live, career moves, or expanding the family.

A Few Other Tidbits about Our Men

Based on my interviews, I'd like to share three more tidbits I learned about from the men:

- Men love marriage
- The serial cheater
- The certified jerk

Men Love Marriage

Yes, it's true: men love marriage. When a man finds "The One," I can assure you he will embrace marriage. Men love the feel and security that comes with being married.

Typically, men remarry rather quickly following a divorce. Why is that? It is because men *love* the feel of marriage. What helps propel men into marriage or remarriage is their lack of analysis over the demise of their previous relationship. Men, for the most part, do not spend much time evaluating why or how the relationship ended, which, in turn, enables them to move forward more quickly following a divorce or breakup.

The Serial Cheater

For every rule, there is an exception. A small percentage of men are going to be perpetual cheaters. Period. It doesn't matter how beautiful and fabulous their partner may be (e.g., Christie Brinkley, Sandra Bullock, and Elin Nordegren). And it doesn't matter how much sex they are having in their marriage; certain men are going to habitually cheat. Serial cheaters are not the men I am writing about in this book. Nor are they, with a few exceptions, the men I interviewed for this book. If you have had an experience with this type of cheater, his behavior is the exception. His ongoing cheating has nothing to do with *you.*

Serial cheater defined: when a man cheats on you more than once, with more than one woman, he is a serial cheater.

You are never going to break into the brain of a serial cheater. You are never going to crack the code of a serial cheater. This type of man is so insecure that successive betrayal of his partner gives him a feeling of self-worth. Another cheating conquest somehow makes him feel like a worthy and wanted man.

Women who are cheated on by a serial cheater must be cautious not to spend years trying to figure out "why" he cheats.

Often, women give chance after chance for the serial cheater to be faithful. In these situations, faithfulness is not going to happen. Take the example of Tiger Woods's ex-wife, Elin Nordegren. She did not spend years trying to unravel the mind of her husband to find out *why* he cheated on her with so many women. Instead, she swiftly left the marriage and moved on with her life in a positive way.

However, there is another type of cheater we need to discuss. It's the cheater who cheated one time. It could be a one-night stand, but most likely, the cheat is with one woman over a period of time. I do not consider this type of cheating to be serial cheating. I do not condone any type of cheating, but we cannot bury our heads in the sand and think all cheating must result in a divorce or breakup. I do not believe in the adage "Once a cheater, always a cheater." My interviews and research have shown this not to be true.

Men, aside from serial cheaters, do not wake up one morning and decide to cheat. Chris's story illustrates this point. Chris is a kind and handsome engineer. I met and spoke with him at length about the reasons some men cheat. Chris shared his personal story with me: He was deeply in love with his wife, but was starved for affection at home. His wife had no interest in sex, and he had to beg her for any sexual attention. Chris explained that their three teenage daughters took up all of his wife's time and attention. Frankly, Chis felt left out and alone.

Chris spoke of the powerful bond his wife would have had with him if she simply had shown some affection and made him feel wanted. Chris stated, "If I had a woman who wanted me—really wanted me—who put me first and made me feel as if she desired me, I would never stray. I would take care of her endlessly. She would be my queen." Chris and his wife divorced six months after our conversation. Chris remarried one year after his divorce.

Many of the men I interviewed admitted that they had previously cheated a single time on their partners. I thought it important to ask about why they cheated and the individual circumstances of the cheat. In most of these cases, they loved their partners. However, their wives or girlfriends either avoided intimacy with them or the cheater perceived himself to be very low on her list of priorities. The men found themselves pleading to have sex with their own wives. In other cases, certain men made an asinine one-time decision to cross a line of trust in the marriage.

I ask you to be extremely cautious about leaving the relationship with the one-time cheater. If his one-event cheating is not something you can forgive or live with, that is understandable, and you have to do what is right for you. However, do not listen to your friends. Do not listen to your coworkers. Do not listen to your family. Listen to your heart, and give your relationship the chance to possibly heal and work through his transgression. If it was a one-event cheat, and both parties want to save the relationship, it certainly may be worth fighting for.

If you are trying to work through a cheating event and you *both* want your relationship to survive and heal, as hard as it may be, learning to let it go is important. I am not suggesting that you wave a wand and erase the hurt and anger from your brain. We are not robots, and of course, feelings of hurt and betrayal are raw and real and must be acknowledged. Take the time you need. If you want to remain together, forgiveness must occur. It won't happen overnight, and it will take a serious effort from both partners to put it in the past and make the necessary changes to grow as a couple.

Why must you move past the cheat in order to save your relationship? Based on my interviews, the men who did have a previous one-time cheat said the lack of letting the event remain in the past is what ultimately ended the relationship for good. Again, only you can determine if the cheating is something you can forgive and ultimately put in the past.

My friend Sam explained his cheating by saying his wife made him feel horrible about himself on a daily basis. After his cheating episode, his wife could not let it go. She complained to Sam about the cheating event for years. She threw the cheating event back at Sam at every turn. A disagreement about dinner plans would turn into an attack about cheating. Sam and Nicole finally broke up for good after eight years together.

My co-worker Doug confessed that he had cheated on his wife after eighteen years of marriage. He was not a serial cheater by any means and fell into the one-event cheat category. The reason Doug gave for cheating on his wife: She grew very cold towards him and had no interest in sex.

Doug didn't plan to cheat. While he was seated alone at a restaurant, a woman a few tables over asked Doug to take a photo of her and her friend. Eventually, Doug ended up sitting at their table, and the woman started showing Doug some attention. Doug was surprised by how lovely it felt to have a little female attentiveness. It reminded him of what he'd been missing from his wife for so many years.

If after the infidelity you would like to save your relationship and move forward, it is crucial to give him the opportunity to prove his devotion to you and regain your trust. The door with "the event" in it is *behind* you, shut and locked. If both parties are committed to rebuilding the partnership, the focus needs to be only on the open door in *front* of you with your budding future of trust and love rebuilding itself.

The Certified Jerk

For every two great guys in the world, there is one jerk of a guy. Hey, it happens. The key is not to spend too much of your precious time on a certified jerk. A handful of men are just lifetime jerks. By lifetime jerk, I mean he has *very* few redeeming qualities. Sure, he can charm the pants off of a snake, but behind that charm and charisma is an ass of a guy. It's in his DNA, and all of our nagging and training and waiting for him to become a good man are an incredible waste of our time.

There are so many good men out there just waiting for a great woman to come into their lives. Every day you spend hoping for a jerk transformation from your guy makes *you* unavailable to meet your non-jerk, hell-of-a-great-guy.

Do not allow yourself to be unavailable to a potentially awesome guy because you have willingly made the choice to wait for your boyfriend or husband to become a great guy. It is not likely going to happen.

If you suffer through each day with a partner you do not want to be with, you have robbed yourself of a day in which you might have met a really wonderful guy. If you're "in a relationship," then you are not available for future good love. If you stay with the lifetime jerk, the energy you expend trying to transform him into a respectable guy is simply negative energy. Use your energy in a more positive way—on *you* and your future. And more importantly, why waste your time trying to reform someone?

One more thing about the jerk. I believe in what is known as the "80/20 rule" for relationships. It's a theory that says, in a healthy relationship, you should be getting approximately 80 percent of the qualities you want in a partner. Maybe your partner isn't the cleanest guy in the world or he's not as affectionate as you may like, but it's okay because the 80 percent you do get from him is really great. Maybe your partner flies off the handle and acts like a three-year-old once a month for a day, but on the other twenty-nine days of the month, he is amazing. Only you can decide whether it is the 80 percent of him or the 20 percent of him that is the jerk.

A warning: Be very careful about ending a relationship of a 20-percent jerk. That 100-percent-perfect partner does not exist. For every 20-percent jerk you release back into the dating pool, there are multiple women who will be lined up to date or marry your man. Trust me, the next man you meet will also come with 20 percent of him that will drive you nuts too.

Let's keep it real here: The 20-percent jerk I am talking about is your standard, everyday, run-of-the mill, jerk-guy behavior that is likely present in every relationship. However, if his 20-percent jerk consists of serial cheating or any physical or emotional abuse, your guy should be history.

The 80/20 rule comes into play only if *you* have true feelings for your partner. If you feel no Dang whatsoever for your partner, then I do not care what your equation is. It does not matter how the math adds up. You cannot make your body feel a love and attraction that is not there. However, if you felt the love in the past and currently your Factor is at a very low level, I do believe you can get that back to where you started as a couple.

7

If we change the way we love, we will love the way we change.

The Women

This chapter is where we get serious about changing the way women love. This chapter is also where we learn to un-love when a relationship does not go according to plan. In this chapter, you will look inward, recognize the areas that may need some adjustments, and reinvent yourself as a woman on a one-way path to home. It will all start to make sense. Every road you have traveled up to this point has led you to where you are meant to be: loved, adored, and blissfully at ease with accepting nothing but good love in your life.

In this chapter about women, you'll come to understand that every bit of heartache, relationship turmoil, and lessons on life has been necessary to get you to the finish line in this crazy game called love. This is where you learn to make peace with yourself (and your ex) so you can freely move forward. Finally, this is where you will say farewell to any lingering ghosts of the past and forge a path to a love-soaked life.

If you are anything like most of the two thousand divorced, separated, or single (as in never-been-married) women I've interviewed, you probably have a plethora of good reasons for everything related to your stalled love life. You married a jerk. He cheated on you. All the good ones are taken. Men are assholes. Dating is too much work. You don't have time to date. I am here to tell you loud and clear: You need to forget all of that. While what you are saying may be true, I promise there is a world of good love out there waiting for you.

Divorce, separation, and being single are the perfect times in your life to shake things up a bit. A woman in transition is a beautiful sight to behold. Maybe you have been solely focused on the kids for many years. Maybe finding a partner has been on the back burner as you focused on your education and building a career. With kids, careers, friends, and financial obligations, it's easy to lose oneself along the way. Reinvention is key, and now is a great time to rearrange your mind, body, and soul to create the life you want.

So where do you start?

Let's begin with eight small, incremental steps designed to shift your focus inward to spark positive change and personal evolution:

- Step 1: Be Woman Strong
- Step 2: Focus on Good Love
- Step 3: Take Responsibility
- Step 4: Embrace Change
- Step 5: Forgive
- Step 6: Adjust Your Breakup Attitude
- Step 7: Beware the Haters
- Step 8: Check the Baggage

Step 1: Be Woman Strong

First and foremost, being "woman strong" means taking control of the way you choose to spend your life coin. It drives me crazy to watch women give up on their desire for adoring love. There is real love out there for every woman on this planet, and it's my mission to help you find yours. Woman smart equals wise spending of your coin. It is making a budget, investing in you, and making purchases according to *your* life plan.

To be woman strong, you need to identify and stay focused on your future. Is it your goal to marry or remarry? Do you want to become a mother? Would you like to have one child or a large family of six? Is it best to break up or divorce, or is your relationship worth trying to save and resurrect the once lustful and deep connection you both felt?

Once you identify your objectives, stay focused and do your best to ignore outside influences—your family, your ex, your friends, what society expects. Whatever *your* vision may be, let your inner woman strength guide your memorable path home.

Step 2: Focus on Good Love

There are two kinds of love: good love and bad love. The difference between the two is black and white. There is no gray area of love. I am an advocate of good love, which looks something like this:

1. Both partners mutually desire each other.
2. Both partners share the same life vision.
3. Good love is reciprocal.
4. Good love does not hurt.
5. Good love moves forward.

Bad love, on the other hand, is just that, and bad love is bad for *you*. Bad love hurts. Bad love is one-sided love and lopsided adoration. Bad love is love without common life goals. Bad love is stagnant love. The last thing I want you to do is to stagnate and not be completely adored by your partner.

Step 3: Take Responsibility

We've all made mistakes. We have all jumped into a relationship too quickly or held onto an unhealthy relationship too long. Missteps and failures hurt, but they are how you learn and grow. As Maya Angelou said, "When you know better, you do better." But to do better, you have to take responsibility.

The key to this step is to recognize that many of your own decisions have led you to this point in life. If you are divorced, it is vital you recognize the role you may have played in the breakup of your marriage. More often than not, *both* parties have contributed in some degree to a collapsed relationship. Accountability is essential for forward momentum.

If you are single or have never married, it is important to recognize that you *may* have some issues you need to work on in the dating department (such as letting the world know you are single and available and putting some time into dating). The crucial first step to the life you want is to take ownership of your love life and its presently stalled and unfulfilled state. And then do something about it.

Life changes. Situations change. Feelings change. Families change. Love changes. He changes. You change. And sometimes, all of the change in your life hurts like hell. Sometimes, the hurt is so bad it rocks you to your core. Sometimes, it's just not fair. Trust me; I know firsthand how a breakup can cause gut-wrenching pain. A breakup or divorce can feel like the blood has drained out of your being. In no way do I minimize how horrible a betrayal or a breakup can be. But I promise you will get through it. The fact is, you *can* and *will* rebuild your life. You will come out of the breakup stronger than ever and thrive beyond belief.

My focus is on you and your future. I promise, with a little reflection and time, you will look back in bewilderment and wonder at how you could have wanted to stay in your past relationships. If you are currently single, someone in your past (possibly you?) did you a huge favor by ending a prior relationship, and you are not going to let *his* life decisions dictate *your* life decisions—especially when it comes to *your* future.

Remember what I told you about the Dang Factor: *It must be mutual.* A one-sided love is no love at all. If someone leaves you for someone else, that person was not the long-term partner for you. And you know what? It's okay. Sometimes love can and will dwindle away. You are not allotted just one love throughout your life. Ideally, sure, it would be great to find your lifetime love, but the reality is, a love evolution will often dictate your life. You cannot force mutual love, nor should you want to.

Step 4: Embrace Change

Positive energy is infectious. For a divorced or single woman, this is your time for revival and rebirth. The possibilities are endless when it comes to your future. *You* are now in control of the road you travel, and it's a one-way highway to happiness. If you're willing to embrace positive change, you hold all the power. I want you to use that power to find your life balance and dictate the new way you're going to love.

Have you any idea how many incredible partners are out there just waiting to fall in love with you? To venture into the next phase of your life, you need to find and welcome inner happiness and bury thoughts of past relationships. Embrace your past relationships and learn from them. Admit your faults and work to correct them. Remember, the people in your past were there for a purpose. Their role in your life was to propel you forward to the next step of your journey.

I want you to use this time in your life to make a change. After a *reasonable* mourning period following your split, it will be time to focus on your future and set up a game plan. I am going to challenge you to make one positive change in your life because change and evolution are good for you. One simple change in your life can work wonders. Change brings forward motion and personal evolution.

You'd be surprised how one simple change can ripple and create a cascade of positivity and opportunity. A new hobby or sport will give you a fresh focus. Change will help to reinvent and rearrange your soul. Change will help you meet new people with similar interests and life goals. Change will mean something *different* in your life.

A good example of making positive change is my friend Gail. Gail recently went through a devastating divorce. Gail was married for twenty years to the man she thought was the love of her life. Gail's husband, Rob, met a woman at work and left the marriage.

After months of tears and a zombie-like existence, Gail made a change: Gail started running. On her first run, Gail ran one block and almost passed out. The next week, she ran two blocks. Each and every week, Gail ran farther. She lost weight. She gained confidence. Within one year, Gail ran her first marathon. Gail's newfound love of running brought a surprise: love. Gail met Andrew, a fellow marathon runner, along the way, and they are now married.

I have several friends who have gone through a divorce and never changed a single thing about themselves. Nothing. Twelve years later, there they are. Same mindset. Same loneliness. Same complaints. The same life they were so unhappily living before, but now minus their ex.

By embracing change, you're able to grab an opportunity to venture out and shake life up a bit. The more change you make from your old life, the more aware you will become of your coin and the way it is spent.

Step 5: Forgive

We all know the story of Tiger Woods and his immense betrayal of his wife, Elin Nordegren. When Elin found out about the serial cheating, she had two choices: She could become a victim, seek revenge, and hate Tiger forever; or she could accept the situation, rebuild her life, and spend her coin on her fabulous future.

Elin chose the second option. This is not to say she was not extremely pissed off and hurt by what her husband had done. Of course, she was. Who wouldn't be? However, in the end, Elin proved to be a woman of class and character and, as a result, has moved on and will have a beautiful and love-filled life.

Elin made the decision not to let her ex-husband retain control of her life coin. Instead, she chose to make peace, move forward, and rebuild her life. After weathering her personal storm, Elin returned to school full time to complete her degree in psychology. Selected as an outstanding graduate, Elin gave the commencement speech at her graduation from Rollins College, saying, "If I can inspire even one mom to go back and get her degree with the message that it's never too late, then I am happy."

When asked in *People* magazine about her life, Nordegren explained, "I have moved on, and I am in a good place. Our relationship is centered around our children, and we are doing really good. We really are. He is a great father."

When asked about Tiger Woods's then-relationship with skier Lindsey Vonn, Nordegren replied, "I'm happy for Tiger. In general, in any kind of stepparent relationship, I'm happy that there's somebody else loving my children."

Elin's mindset is incredible, and her outlook on life is the reason she has moved forward. Quite simply, Elin refused to let her anger toward her ex dictate *her* future. Elin also kept the best interests of her children in the forefront of her mind.

In similar fashion, Jennifer Garner also chose the second option following her split from Ben Affleck.

In a 2016 interview with *Vanity Fair,* she said, "It's not Ben's job to make me happy. The main thing is these kids—and we're completely in line with what we hope for them. Sure, I lost the dream of dancing with my husband at my daughter's wedding. But you should see their faces when he walks through the door. And if you see your kids love someone so purely and wholly, then you're going to be friends with that person." She added, "No one needs to hate him for me. I don't hate him."

We cannot think for one minute that Garner's breakup has not been brutally painful. But in the end, Jennifer made the choice to steer her own ship by forgiving and moving forward with grace.

Be honest. If you were a guy, wouldn't you just love to be with someone like Jennifer or Elin, both of whom have such refreshing attitudes about their exes? And yes, I understand that these examples are both of women with celebrity status and money. But don't dismiss their cases outright because of that. Think of all the other messy public divorces of celebrities with money that have played out in the headlines. Both women easily could have chosen the path of hatred and revenge. Instead, both women made the choice to forge a different path down a positive and productive road.

The Letter of Peace

All new life journeys should begin with peace. You must make peace with your past, so it will not screw up your future. If you carry past anger and animosity with you into your new life adventure, you will not get far. The Letter of Peace is a means of letting go of your past and opening the gate to a brand new world. Simply put, until your Gate of Peace is opened, your future love life could be effectively closed.

I promise you, the Letter of Peace will change your world. The Letter of Peace is a self-proclamation that will propel you forward in life. It is the art of letting go of the history of a love that did not go according to plan. If a former partner is a topic of your conversation some two, five, ten, or twenty years post-breakup, then he has maintained a hold on you that you need to shake off. Thinking about him so far after your split demonstrates the power and control he has continued to have over you.

I understand you may have reason to be angry; however, anger is *your* roadblock. I don't want you to allow the frustration you feel toward an ex to rob you of future love. Yes, he may be a no-good son-of-a-bitch. In fact, he probably is. Yes, you may think he is the worst human being on the planet. But, at one point in your life, you built a relationship with this person. At one time, you liked this person enough to have sex with him. Maybe you even created beautiful children with him. The fact is, *something* good likely came from that relationship.

Making mental peace with your ex is an excellent tool to move you forward. Write him a letter. Write him an email. Send him a text. I don't care how you do it. Just do it. In fact, I don't even care if you deliver the message to him. Just write it, absorb it, and mean it.

Often, we act out against our exes because we are mad at ourselves. Maybe we should have tried harder. Maybe we regret leaving him. Maybe we miss him. Maybe we made a mistake. Maybe he was not the best choice in a partner. Maybe our mistake was staying in the relationship too long. Maybe we are angry with him for moving on so quickly after the breakup.

Write the letter that will change your life. Accept the fact that you both may have contributed to the demise of your relationship. Recognize that you may not have been a good fit for each other for the long haul. Acknowledge that each of you may not have been focused on the relationship. Accept that he was not a good long-term match for your life desires.

Whatever the reason for the breakup, embrace it. Learn from it. Rejoice in it. When you enter your next life phase with peace, your path to love will explode with possibilities.

The Letter of Peace will change not only your life but also the lives of your children, family, and friends, who are likely caught in the crossfire of the split. When children are involved, it is the parents' behavior *after* the relationship ends that sets the scene for the rest of their lives.

Sample Letter of Peace

Dear [Your Ex]:

I am writing you this letter as an offer of peace between the two of us. We did not work out as a forever couple, and I now realize we both played a role in our breakup. I am taking responsibility for my actions that led to our marriage/relationship crumbling. Our divorce/breakup was not entirely your fault, although I may have acted as if it were only your fault for many years.

Looking back on our marriage/relationship, I realize I may not have been the best wife, partner, friend, and lover that I could have been. I also understand, as time passed, we grew apart and ultimately did not share the same life dreams and expectations.

I do not want to fight with you any longer. I apologize for my actions of the past. Please accept my letter of peace. I wish you the best.

Sincerely,

[The New You]

Step 6: Adjust Your Breakup Attitude

The way you react to the breakup sets the scene for your future. Remember, love must be reciprocal. The last thing I ever want you to do is to try to convince your partner to love you. Remind yourself that your breakup partner is simply your guiding star whose purpose was to propel you forward and lead you to embrace nothing less than *mutual* love in your life.

For the longest time we women have had it all wrong. Think about it: Men expect women to act argumentative and outraged after the breakup. When you react to a breakup in a calm and dignified manner, it leaves men shocked and confused. With your new breakup attitude, he will be scratching his head and always wondering if he did the right thing by letting go of such an ultra-classy lady.

Do your best to be civil post-breakup. Resist the urge to leave scathing messages on his voicemail. Resist the urge to talk poorly about him to your children, family, and friends. (You could end up getting back together, so no need to advertise what a jerk he is.) Resist the urge to destroy his belongings. Fight the urge to yell at him. (Okay, maybe one really good scream, but no more!)

Breakups are damn hard. Trust me, I have been there. I know it can feel like your guts have been ripped out. You can't eat. You can't sleep. But here's the deal: you must go through the pain to get over the pain. And it hurts like hell. But you will survive each day, second by second, as you begin to turn your stagnant pain into productive pain.

Productive pain is beneficial to you and your future. Productive pain is pain you must feel in order to benefit from it. Productive pain is channeling your pain into positive changes and growth. It is pain that produces beneficial results to your life. It is pain that pulls you into its fire and ultimately leads you to discover you are, in fact, fireproof.

In the meantime, you have moved on, sister. Be strong. Be dignified and walk away from the relationship with your head held high. If you run into your ex, be cordial. No need to hate the guy. He just did you an awesome favor. Your breakup attitude determines your future altitude. The sooner you begin your journey forward, the sooner you soar.

Do not dwell on the whys or what-ifs of the breakup. Take the whys and learn from them for future self-improvement and growth. Take action to rebirth yourself. Keep your breakup off social media. And no, you do not need to be Facebook friends.

A gracious breakup is a good breakup. *(More on this is coming in Chapter 9: The Breakup.)*

Avoid the A-Syndrome

What is the A-Syndrome? The A-Syndrome is post-breakup behavior that will stop your life in its tracks. The A-Syndrome is behaving in a way that is unacceptable on every level. It is behavior destructive to not only you but also those closest to you.

The A-Syndrome is a post-breakup reaction filled with so much anger and animosity toward an ex that any possible leap toward a renewed love life is crushed before it can begin to blossom. It is dislike toward an ex that is so obsessive and unhealthy that it consumes life.

The key is to replace the anger of the A-Syndrome with drive and ambition to change your life and achieve your dreams. Yes, he turned out to be a schmuck, but if you feel anything but pure indifference toward him (after a *reasonable* amount of time has passed), he will continue to have spending rights to your life coin. Your energy needs to be spent on your future, not on your past.

Another toxic prong of the A-Syndrome is your children. Your children must not be used as a way to get back at an ex. This is by far the most destructive and damaging behavior any divorced or single parent could engage in. Parental alienation is real. A custody battle for the sake of "winning" is poison to you and your children's future. Your love for your children and their well-being must rise above your distaste for their father.

Step 7: Beware the Haters

Once you begin to disassemble and reinvent your life, I must warn you: You will have haters. You will lose many of your so-called "friends." Why? Because your friends, who are miserable in their relationships, want you to be just as miserable as they are.

Many women you thought were your friends will no longer speak with you. Instead, your "friends" may talk about you behind your back and just be downright nasty. It's okay. You will make new and better friends who will support your happiness.

If you take charge of your coin and seek satisfying happiness, it will cost you. The risk of being happy may cost you a friend or two. Your happiness may even cost you a family member or two. Why? Because certain people in your life are not going to be supportive of your journey. Those same people will not want you to find love and live a passion-filled life. Why? Because *they* are not happy, and *your* experiencing newfound feelings of bliss makes them jealous.

Losing a couple of "friends" in your pursuit of a blissful life is a small price to pay. During my journey, I came to realize that some people are just happy being miserable. These same people want to grow old and complain about their empty and lonely lives. They want to complain about their lack of desire for sex and their distaste for their partner. More importantly, they want you to complain with them. When you are no longer a participant in their unhappiness club, your "friends" may frown upon your happiness.

On the flip side, you will keep and flourish in the real friendships and relationships of the people who want you to be happy.

They'll marvel at your newfound zest for life; they'll encourage you and support your journey to love. They will stand by you and celebrate your happiness. You may even inspire a friend or relative to make a change in his or her own life. Stay focused on the people in your life who accept your journey without judgment and truly care about your bliss.

Step 8: Check the Baggage

"Baggage" is certainly a term that can make both men and women run the other direction when venturing into a new relationship. For the most part, we all have baggage. The key is to ask yourself *what kind* of baggage you bring to your new relationship. The vast majority of the men I interviewed had no problem with baggage, per se. After all, men are equally baggage prone after a split, and we *all* had a life well before we met someone new.

What we *do not* want is *bitter baggage*. Bitter baggage is our leftover disdain for an ex. Bitter baggage is animosity toward an ex that needs to be left curbside as you venture into the world of love. Bitter baggage is when the focus is to "get back" at someone or financially destroy a previous partner. It is resorting to parental alienation to destroy the relationship your children have with the other parent.

Note: Children are never baggage. In my case, my new husband took on all four of my kids as if they were his own. Do not think for one second that being a mother will stop you from finding love. Most men love kids and will welcome yours with open arms.

One Last Thing: Marriage Matters

For women who are currently married, I want to share something with you. Most marriages break up because the couples simply grow apart. Most divorces come about when one or both parties stop putting in the effort needed to keep a marriage strong and healthy. I firmly believe the majority of marriages with a morsel of Dang left in them can be saved and brought back to life.

I asked thousands of men to pinpoint the reason their marriage dissolved. Each one said the same thing: He left the marriage (or cheated) because the connection to his partner had broken. The affection, once so strong, ceased. The sex stopped. He was no longer a priority. She stopped trying and, in return, he did too (or vice versa).

The men explained how much they crave a close physical connection to their partner. In each case, once the sexual intimacy left, so did the closeness and special bond these men felt for their partners. I encourage you to use the power of sex and seduction to keep your marriage spicy hot, because marriage matters. Especially yours.

The following question was posed to a group of women whose partners travel for work. As you read their answers, you will see some of the women put the effort into their love life with their partner. Others, well, not so much.

Where would you fall in line with your answer? Do you still "primp" for your partner? Keep in mind that these ladies had days or weeks without their partner, and many of them put *zero* effort in before his homecoming. Marriage takes work. Marriage takes effort. Marriage requires staying sexually connected, far beyond the day you said, "I do."

Here is the question asked of the women:

> How many of you ladies primp and prepare before your guy comes home after a work trip? Mine is home Friday after being away for two weeks. Every time it seems like the week of his coming home it's pedicure, hair, shave, and getting our bedroom ready. I guess I look forward to looking good. How about you?

Here's how they responded:

> Christine: *I definitely do that. I enjoy it immensely.*
>
> Sarah: *With my twins in middle school, I am happy just to take a shower before my husband comes home. Someday maybe I will primp again!*
>
> Cheryl: *My husband is lucky if I shave my legs and get out of my bathrobe.*
>
> Autumn: *It depends. If he gets home on a night when the kids aren't home or are in bed, I tend to go all out. Last week, he had been gone for a week, and we did not have any kids for the night. I greeted him all done up with my shortest dress on, heels,*

sitting on the kitchen counter with a cocktail in hand. He's been raving about that homecoming all week! Now, if he gets home in the middle of my workday and I've been rushing kids here and there, I don't do as much!

Jennifer: *Legs shaved and a clean house. I throw in a meal from time to time.*

Melanie: *Yep, I would do that, including making sure the house was clean, the refrigerator was full, and it included his favorite foods/snacks. And the bedroom was definitely ready.*

Heather: *Absolutely. It keeps the spark alive and keeps the interest on each other. I have read many articles that say we need to put spouses above everything, including kids. Effort is always a good thing! Plus, men are super visual.*

Sara: *I was just thinking this morning as I got all dolled up because my hubby was coming home from a five-day trip about how much money I must save on makeup now that my husband is working out of town. I swear my makeup is only done on days he is home. I also only wear my cute clothes when he's home. Days when he's gone it's no makeup and yoga pants.*

Marie: *Never. Those days of looking nice are over.*

Stacey: *I have two on-the-go kiddos and a dog. They come first. He is lucky if he has a cold beer in the fridge.*

Linda: *All the time.*

Rachel: *I used to when he was gone two months at a time. I would always look extra nice to pick him up at the airport. Now that he is home every night, I don't need to bother.*

Megan: *I always primp, pluck, and shave before he comes home. Even though he's doing five days on right now, we both enjoy keeping that spark going.*

Rose: *No way. I have the same routine every day, and it does not involve primping or makeup. I am not going to change my routine because he came home from work. Of course, I did primp before we got married, but no more.*

Natasha: *I love to primp before I see him!*

Nancy: *Eleven years married, and I stopped the primping after the first year. Now it's normal for me to have on an old t-shirt and sweats when he comes in.*

Lisa: *I try to remember to shave. But to be honest, half the time he walks in the door, and I say, "Oh, I didn't know you were coming home today!" It's the kiddos that are first for us right now.*

Stella: *Always.*

Christine: *On my days off, he's lucky if I get out of my pajamas. I primp for work, but not for him. No kids, but I doubt I would have time for primping with an infant to look after.*

Cathy: *A tip if you forgot to shave: Victoria's Secret thigh-high hose. My husband loves them!*

Liz: *Married fifteen years and I, too, am over primping. That lasted the first few years. Having kids was a great excuse to say goodbye to primping.*

Julie: *I'd say he has a 50/50 shot at catching me on a shower day. I have two kids. I'm not even sure where my makeup bag is these days, and I don't plan to ever find it.*

Well, there you have it. Some of the answers were so refreshing to read, and others, unfortunately, demonstrated the sad reality of many marriages. The latter also explain the 50 percent divorce rate in the United States and the cheating epidemic that runs rampant in marriages.

I get it. We get married, and we get comfortable. Comfort is a good thing to an extent. However, comfort should not replace effort from either partner. As the years go by, it is vital to make an effort to at least semi-resemble the person each of you married.

Getting too comfortable in marriage and losing the desire to put in the effort is a danger zone I do not want either of you to enter. Your marriage needs to come first. When you and your partner are connected and close, everything else will fall into place.

"I do" should never turn into "I don't"—from either partner.

8

The decisions we make while dating will lead to lasting consequences. If we are woman wise, we are woman strong.

The Date Wise Meter

Ever been to an amusement park or arcade and played the high striker? It's that attraction where you use a mallet to test your strength in order to win a prize. If you hit the base hard enough, it will cause a puck to shoot upward toward a bell. The closer you get to ringing the bell, the "stronger" you are. Now imagine a meter that measures how "wise" your dating and relationship skills are. Instead of strength, we are testing your knack for making life choices that will lead you to discover and embrace good love.

That's what this chapter is all about. How high or low would your puck rise on the Date Wise Meter? To help you hit the base harder and send that puck higher, I've included nine lessons to help raise your relationship IQ:

Lesson 1: Let Life Goals Dictate Spending Habits

Lesson 2: Recognize Red Flags Early

Lesson 3: Don't Exit the Dating Pool Too Soon

Lesson 4: Date Like a Dude

Lesson 5: Burst the Bubble

Lesson 6: Beware of the Relationship Rearview Mirror

Lesson 7: Listen to the "No" to Marriage or Children

Lesson 8: Monitor your Timeline

Lesson 9: Build Progressive Commitment

The following lessons are all based on true stories. As you read each lesson, stay focused on where you would fall on our dating and relationship meter. Compare these women's stories with your past or present relationships. Learn from our sisters' missteps and successes, and make their lessons your own.

Lesson 1: Let Life Goals Dictate Spending Habits

Your life vision—be it college, career, marriage, remarriage, or children—should dictate your dating and relationship spending habits. I want you to ask yourself what *your* goals are and develop a plan to stick to them. I'm not here to tell you what *you* want out of your life. Instead, I am here to make you aware that inattentive spending can result in undesirable consequences.

My friend Anna has been a huge inspiration for *The Dang Factor*. Over the past ten years, I have watched in despair as Anna has generously given, and has continued to give away, days, months, and years of her coin to men who have no intention of making a long-term commitment to her.

First and foremost, Anna wants to remarry. Now, it's not that Anna doesn't date; it's that she doesn't spend wisely on the men she does date. Divorced for thirteen years, Anna has lost sight of her objective and has wasted far too many pennies on men who have no intention to marry.

Anna started her journey to remarriage when she was thirty-eight years old. Now, at age fifty-one, Anna is no closer to finding a meaningful relationship that will lead to her goal of remarriage. Instead, Anna has continued to give away precious years of her life to men who clearly are not interested in the same life goals as she.

Following her divorce, Anna dated Kevin for *two years*. While dating Kevin, Anna lived in San Diego and Kevin lived in Los Angeles. Anna and Kevin were both upfront when they met that neither would be willing to move from his or her respective city. After two years, Kevin broke up with Anna. Kevin has since married a woman from Los Angeles.

Anna then started dating Steve. Anna gave Steve *three years* of her coin. When Anna started dating Steve, Anna's children were teenagers, and Anna was not interested in having more children. In fact, she had had her tubes tied after her youngest child was born. Steve, however, desperately wanted to have babies. After three years of dating, Steve broke off their relationship to focus on finding a wife he could make babies with. Steve is now married and is the father of two children.

Anna's next boyfriend, Adam, was perfect for Anna, as they worked in the same profession and shared the same work schedule (summers off). They lived—and wanted to stay—in the same small town. Neither Adam nor Anna wanted more children. So Adam and Anna dated. And they dated. And they dated. *Four years* of dating, and still no commitment from Adam.

Anna has allowed so many years of her life to be given away to men who were perfectly content just to date her. When Anna brought up the subject of marriage—after four years of dating—Adam broke off the relationship.

Jeff is Anna's current boyfriend. Jeff also happens to be legally married to someone else. Anna and Jeff have been dating for *three years.* Jeff spends most nights at Anna's house. You know the saying: Why buy the cow when you get the milk for free? Anna has now been giving out *free milk* for *thirteen years* to men who have no intention to marry her.

If you want to become a mom or you want to marry or remarry, your coin is crucial. I cannot tell you the number of women who have wanted so badly to become mothers and spent countless years with a man who did not want children. Sadly, many of these women are now too old to have children. Please do not let your partner take away your precious childbearing years, if motherhood is something you desire.

My friend Lauren was married to Rob for eighteen years. During the marriage, Lauren begged Rob to start a family. Rob, already a father of two children, was adamant about not having more kids with Lauren. Lauren decided it was better to be with Rob, who was the "love of her life," than to leave the marriage and find a man who wanted a family. Lauren painfully gave up her dream of motherhood to stay in her marriage.

When Lauren turned forty-eight, Rob ended the marriage. And yes, as you might have guessed, Rob remarried and is now the father of two more children. Lauren, now fifty-three years old, has remained single and childless.

I want you to be able to look back and know you have achieved *your* dreams and goals. Don't allow someone to take away your dreams of love, marriage, motherhood, and family.

I know it's emotionally difficult to leave or move on from a relationship. I've felt the immense pain of a breakup, and I know how hard it is. However, looking back at a life void of mutual adoring love and missed life dreams is even more difficult.

Don't be afraid to leave a relationship that clearly does not fit your dreams. Your courage must be bigger than your fear of being alone. To be alone opens your world to the possibilities of finding the person who will enhance your life and help to create your unbridled happiness.

Lesson 2: Recognize Red Flags Early

Your Date Wise Meter will rise if you learn to recognize relationship red flags early. Yes, the sex may be fantastic, but if his life goals don't match your goals, it's simply a waste of your time, energy, and effort.

Another friend, Janel, has made significant progress following her ten-plus years of poor dating decisions. Janel wants to be married. Janel began her dating journey at the age of fifty. Now she is sixty years old. A light bulb finally turned on, and the reality of possibly never marrying has set in.

When I last spoke with Janel, she had made enormous progress in her dating decisions. Recently, Janel had been seeing a man she was quite attracted to. He lived ten hours away from Janel (red flag), and he has three small children (another red flag). However, the good news is Janel recognized early on they were not a long-term match.

Janel's Date Wise Meter clicked on, and she broke things off. Was this a difficult decision for Janel to make? Yes. Was it painful? Hell, yes. However, Janel was quick to recognize that she does not want to spend time in a long-distance relationship, nor does she want to raise three small children at the age of sixty. Janel saw the red flags, acted on them, and is now available and back in the dating game, where she can focus on finding good love and remarriage.

Lesson 3: Don't Exit the Dating Pool Too Soon

Men love to have you be exclusive with them right away. After one date, many men will ask you to delete your online dating profile. Why? They want you out of the dating arena and available only to them. Don't do this in haste. It's up to *you* to set your dating boundaries.

Remember, once you commit to a relationship that clearly has no future, you're *off* the dating market and unavailable to meet your future love. Be careful of the manipulative skills of the men you are dating. Men are talented at getting you to come back to them, so it's vital you date smart early on. If you become or remain emotionally connected to a man you have no future with, it will be very difficult to break away and move forward.

Why do we stay? We get comfortable. We think our guy will change. We are scared to be alone. Trust me, I've made these same mistakes. Luckily, I pulled myself out of my dead-end relationships and gave away only a few years of my coin. Fortunately, I was young enough to afford it, and I had already had my children, so becoming a mom was not an issue. The one thing I did know for sure was that I wanted to remarry at some point in my life. So I jumped back into the dating pool, smarter and focused on my goal. I tailored my dating accordingly and made better dating choices, which ultimately led me to my Dang.

Lesson 4: Date Like a Dude

Something that helped propel me forward into smarter dating was a piece of advice from a friend of mine. After my divorce, she watched me give away three years of my life to a man who was clearly not my Dang, and advised me to "date like a dude." When I asked her what the heck that meant, she explained that men have a different dating philosophy than women. Men, unless they are unequivocally certain *you* are "The One," keep their options open during the dating period. So, instead of dating just you, he may be dating several other women or at least be open to the possibility of doing so by keeping one eye open for your possible replacement.

After I had given away years of my coin by dating exclusively at the onset of each new dating relationship, I decided to do just that: Date like a dude. The date-like-a-dude philosophy is a game changer. It is a beautiful mindset to have when you enter the world of dating.

Dating like a dude allows you to keep your options open and play the field, so to speak. Dating like a dude also keeps you moving forward in the dating world instead of giving your entire being to one guy who may not be your Dang or who has no intention of settling down with you.

Note: Dating like a dude doesn't mean you are to sleep with each and every guy you date. That's where our "Dude Factor" differs from a true dude. Like it or not, there's a double standard between men and women as far as having sex early with multiple partners in the dating process.

Here's the problem: If you have sex right away, he may get possessive, and you may get emotionally attached. If you are emotionally attached, you will not date smart. If you do decide to have sex with one of the men you are seeing, keep the sex to one man only and then keep your options open until you have a clear idea of what direction any exclusive relationship might be headed in.

My "Date Like a Dude" Story

After spending three years of my coin on a couple of dead-end relationships, I decided to try out my friend's theory. I mean, why not, right? I activated my online dating profile, and I was ready to roll. As I scrolled through my emails and "winks," I felt liberated. I was excited for my future because I was going to date like a dude and leave my female emotional attachment at the curb.

I realized that by dating like a dude, I did not have to commit to the first guy who asked me to date him exclusively. Instead, I could have fun along my dating path by meeting many men, committing to no one, and being smart about my future relationship choices. I was ready to have fun; and if my Dang happened along the way, that would be icing on the cake.

My first week of dating like a dude was incredible. I had lined up ten, yes, *ten* dates for week one. (Don't hate: A girl has to do what a girl has to do.) I had a coffee date each morning and a wine date each evening. I met a few fabulous men and a few, um, not so fabulous. But, hey, that's why they call it dating, right? And guess what? The first man I "dated like a dude" is now my incredible husband.

Dating like a dude is a mindset that is empowering and radiates positive energy from you. It is a mindset of independence that attracts men to you like a magnet. But remember, unless you put yourself out there, through online dating or the like, men will have no clue that the sexy and sassy *you* exists and is available.

Dating isn't easy. It's work. It requires putting the time in so you can find your partner and experience beautiful love. So, here's a newsflash: you have to go through it to get over it. Yes, you need to date the creeps and the losers. Yes, you need to put on some makeup and have a conversation with someone other than your dog. Stop putting it off. Stop the excuses. Isn't your future worth it?

Lesson 5: Burst the Bubble

Let's talk about something that happens to a lot of women who aren't in a mutually adoring relationship. I call it "the bubble."

When a woman is in a bubble, she cannot see outside of her dating decisions. Her friends and family recognize the unwise dating decisions, but a person in the bubble will see only perfect, hopeful, and committed love.

Maybe you have been in a bubble yourself. I know I was in a bubble at one time in my dating life, and thankfully I found my way out. I'm sure you know someone in a dating bubble right now. You watch in disbelief at the choices your friend makes about her current relationship.

We can tell our bubble friends how awful their current partner is or how he isn't the one for them, but our warnings will fall on deaf ears. They are trapped in their bubble and simply cannot see out. We can tell them until we are blue in the face what a creep they're dating, but they cannot see it. Nothing, and I mean nothing, will get them out of the bubble, except coming to the harsh realization on their own.

If the bubble is ever going to burst, it has to be on her terms and when she is ready. It may take years, but generally speaking, the bubble of a bad relationship will eventually burst. Most often, it's an outside event that breaks the bubble. The jerk she's dating eventually does something so outrageous that she finally breaks away.

"I cannot believe I was with that guy!" is usually the first response when a woman's bubble bursts. She'll scold you with, "You should have told me how awful he was." Your response:

"I did!" Once she's out of the bubble, the key, of course, is not to enter into another relationship that puts her into another bubble.

Caution: Try like hell to stay out of the dating bubble. Once you enter your bubble, it's an emotionally dangerous place to be. Entering a dating bubble strips you of years of your life that you can never recover. If you are in the bubble, only you can find your way out.

Stacey's Bubble

Stacey is amazing, the total package. She is smart, beautiful, financially secure, funny, and fun. I love this woman, and it makes me crazy to watch her make poor dating choices. Stacey would love to be married. She has been divorced for more than twenty years.

During those twenty years, Stacey focused on her career, which involved traveling all over the world. Consequently, that left little time for dating. As a flight attendant, Stacey dedicated her career to serving others. The problem is, she forgot to serve herself along the way. Stacey is now sixty-five years old. It isn't too late to find love. But time waits for no woman, and her life clock keeps ticking.

Now retired, Stacey was excited to begin seriously dating and find her partner to spend her life with. We made her a Match.com profile and launched her into the world of online dating. The winks and emails poured in. Why wouldn't they? She's incredible. But Stacey brushed off the possibilities of love and instead started having sex with an old friend with whom she had absolutely no future. "Too much effort to date," Stacey complained.

So she did what was comfortable. When I scolded her for her decision, Stacey replied, "But the sex is incredible!"

For "incredible sex," Stacey is spending her precious time on a man who is underemployed, lives with his mother, and has no intention of getting married. Ever. Because Stacey started a sexual relationship with him, two years later she is now emotionally paralyzed in it.

Stacey is in her bubble, and she cannot yet break away. Logically, she knows she needs to break off the relationship, but emotionally, she has been sucked in. And that's a position I do not want to see you in.

Exciting Update on Stacey

I recently received the following message from Stacey:

Michelle: Because of your never-ending persistence and endless lectures about my life coin and finding my Dang, I am finally on the same road to love as you. I am so happy! I broke away from the dating rut I was in and met the man of my dreams. (Yes, online.) I am engaged! *Thank you a million times. I now know what you meant by Good Love. Love you, My Sweet Friend.*

Lesson 6: Beware of the Relationship Rearview Mirror

Out of the thousands of woman I interviewed, a pattern emerged. Years after a difficult breakup or divorce, many women were trapped in the past. Still either in love with their past partner or greatly affected by the breakup, they were stuck looking in the relationship rearview mirror. With their focus on the past, reliving what could have been or what went wrong, these women cut themselves off from any future meaningful love.

The issue for my friend Khloe, as with so many women, is that she is still very attached to her ex. Logically, Khloe knows she needs to move forward with her life. That's the hard part. This is where your heart has to take a back seat to your head if you are to achieve your life goals.

In Khloe's case, her goal is to be remarried and start a family. As Khloe continues to spend years of her life pining away for her now ex-husband, her coin has been spent looking backward, which is not the direction she should be moving in.

The Question

With each new guy Khloe dates, I ask her the same question: *If* he wants to marry you and start a family with you, what will your answer be? Khloe's response is always the same: "I don't think so." My response is always the same: "Then why, oh why, do you continue to date him?"

If, after dating for a reasonable amount of time, your answer to an anticipated proposal is not an unequivocal "Yes," then you need to move on. I want you to step back and think about your past, present, and future relationship choices. You have a window of life that I need you to be extremely cautious about.

Your life window I am focusing on is age thirty and older. After age thirty, your love life becomes a different arena. After age thirty, your body, mind, and soul have a clock that you need to pay very close attention to. Obviously, you know what I mean about your body clock (eggs and baby making), but what about mind and soul? The clock of your mind and soul is a different kind of clock.

As we age, we get more set in our ways. As we age, we like to do things "our way," without input from others. As we age, we can often lose the art of compromise. As we age, we forget how to "play well with others," and it is quite common to become what I call "un-marriable." Do not let yourself become un-marriable because you have lost the ability to cohabitate and compromise. You are way too fabulous for that.

Lesson 7: Listen to the "No" to Marriage or Children

As Maya Angelou famously said, "The first time someone shows you who they are, believe them." If a man tells you that he doesn't want to be married or a father, believe him.

Don't spend years trying to convince him to change his mind. It rarely works and is an enormous waste of your time and energy.

This was my friend Julia's problem. The guy she has been dating for eight years has *no* interest in marriage. Julia is divorced and has already achieved her goal of motherhood, so that is not an issue. The issue is this: Julia wants to get married. Her man does not. That sounds fairly black and white, right? Except Julia is wallowing in the gray area of her relationship when there is no gray to be found.

In Julia's situation, her partner has been upfront and honest with her. He has not led her on. He has not made false promises. He has made it very clear he is not going to get married. So, after eight years of dating, Julia finally broke things off for good.

Do you really want to spend years of your coin on a man who has *no* interest in marrying you? Do you really want to spend years of your life coin hoping to convince someone to make a serious commitment? Are you going to give away years of your life waiting on your man to change his mind and suddenly get down on bended knee? No answer is your answer. Never put yourself in the position of having to beg or convince your man to commit to a life with you.

Lesson 8: Monitor Your Timeline

Heidi's story is the classic tale of a coin being spent on the wrong purchase. It is not so much the initial purchase as it is the *length* of Heidi's purchase that drives me bananas.

When Heidi was twenty-one years old, she met a man and fell in love. After a few years of dating, Heidi and her man moved in together. They lived together for fourteen years. Yes, fourteen big ones, with no commitment. Just as year fifteen approached, Heidi's guy met a woman at work, moved out of their home, and married his new love within nine months. Heidi spent fourteen years auditioning for the role of wife and never got the part.

Here's the deal: I am perfectly fine if you want to live together with your partner. Sure, why not try it out? See if you are compatible. Give things a trial run before saying, "I do." However, if your relationship goal is to eventually be married, it is important for you to have a *reasonable* timeline in mind as to how long you are willing to maintain the live-in-girlfriend status.

Luckily, Heidi is young enough to recover from her dating mishap. However, Heidi's future relationship decisions need to be conducted in a wiser fashion if she is to achieve her goals. Heidi still has time (if she stays focused) to meet her true partner and have the houseful of babies she so desperately desires in her life.

You can make purchases to your heart's desire; just make certain your purchases are sound. Remember, there are no money-back guarantees with a bad relationship purchase. That's why you need to spend your valued coin wisely and efficiently.

If you would like to be married at some point, then you need to have a mental cutoff in your mind of how long you will interview for the role of wife.

A good rule of thumb I like to use when starting to date someone new is to allow three to four dates with your new connection. If, after three or four dates, you know you would definitely not marry this person, I think it is wise to cut off the dating with that person. Why? Because you should not waste your time on someone you *know* you have no future with.

Don't date just for something to occupy your time and satisfy your boredom. Number one, it can make you become emotionally attached to that person, and most importantly, number two, it keeps you out of the dating pool and unavailable to meet the partner you *would* commit to!

Valerie's Story

Valerie's story is a little bit easier to absorb simply because of her age. When Valerie was nineteen years old, she became seriously involved with her twenty-year-old military boyfriend—so serious that, for the next nine years, Valerie moved with her boyfriend to six different states, depending on where he was stationed. Valerie left her family and friends behind and devoted her life to her man and his military career.

For nine years, Valerie and her man talked about the day they would get married and the number of children they would have. The problem: It was just talk. No action. While Valerie uprooted herself from state to state to devote herself to her man and his career, in reality, she was the only one devoted to the relationship. Valerie was simply her man's companion to get him through each move. Yes, as you might have guessed, while in the middle of their latest move to Florida, Valerie was dumped via text message. Her man had met someone at work and ended the relationship.

Valerie still has time for future relationships and commitments. I was very pleased when Valerie's man ended the relationship. Why? Because I am confident that Valerie would have gone along with the "let's just live together" life plan and robbed herself of her dreams of marriage and motherhood for many years to come.

I'm going to give it to you straight: You cannot give away years of your life. You simply do not have that many years to squander. If you are thirty or older and you're marriage or baby minded, you must have some clear sense of the direction in which your relationship is going.

I like to use the nine-month time frame as a measure of direction. If you are dating your partner exclusively for nine months and talk of your future has not come up, you likely need to evaluate whether you share the same life goals. After nine months of exclusive dating, both of you should have a pretty good inclination as to whether this person could be your future spouse.

Stephanie's Story

Stephanie is twenty-seven years old and has been dating Josh for nine years. Stephanie and Josh were high school sweethearts and continued their exclusive relationship throughout college. After graduating from college several years ago, both Stephanie and Josh secured great jobs.

Although Stephanie had hoped for a proposal over the holidays, Josh instead suggested they move in together. Stephanie and Josh are now living together. Josh gets lots of sex with Stephanie now tucked in next to him each night, and he has Stephanie to help pay half the rent and bills. Talk about a win-win for Josh!

Stephanie will now spend the next several years of her life coin as she continues to wait for a proposal. Remember, after an eleven-year investment, if things do not work out, Stephanie is back to square one.

Stephanie's situation is a common one. Let's face it; many couples live together before marriage. The million-dollar question is this: At what point have you dated and lived together long enough? When do you say enough is enough and reclaim your coin?

The answer, of course, centers on your life goals. I want you to be able to look back at your life and celebrate the fact that you did not give up your dreams of marriage and children at the discretion of someone else. I want you to look back and rejoice at beautiful and committed love in your life!

Kayla's Award

Kayla gets my all-time "date smart" award. At the tender age of just twenty-six, Kayla made a hard life choice and ended a three-year relationship with her live-in boyfriend. It was incredibly hard for Kayla to leave the man she truly believed was the love of her life.

What impressed me about Kayla was her maturity to think with her head about her future and stay true to herself and her life goals. Kayla, although crazy about her then-boyfriend, had come to the harsh realization that three crucial elements were missing for a future with him. First, he did not want children. Second, he was not on the same religious path as Kayla. Third, he would not relocate to her home state.

Kayla moved out of their apartment with just her suitcase full of clothes and a pain in the pit of her stomach. But she did it. She and her ex-boyfriend remained on good terms (after all, he did nothing wrong; they were simply not a long-term match), and he tried to beg her back multiple times. However, this girl is one tough cookie. Several times, she came close to running back to him, but she stayed busy and fought the urge.

Several months later, her urge to reunite was minimal. And then it happened: Kayla met an incredible guy at her gym who shares her religious values, wants to have a houseful of children, and is open to relocating someday. It remains to be seen if he is "The One," but Kayla's smart dating style is a step in the right direction to love.

Trust me. I know it's painful. It hurts like hell when a relationship you believed in falls apart. But I promise you, that pain in your stomach will go away, and the light will begin to shine at the other end of the breakup tunnel.

Remember, every relationship that doesn't work out moves you one step closer to the relationship that *will* work out.

Lesson 9: Build Progressive Commitment

My best example of how things with the right partner should progress involves George Clooney, the self-proclaimed perpetual bachelor. George's courtship of his wife, Amal, fits squarely into my rule of commitment. I think most of us would have believed he would never marry again, based on his dating history and aversion to remarriage. Over the past twenty-plus years, George averaged a new girlfriend every couple of years, with none of the relationships culminating in marriage.

Enter Amal Alamuddin, a smart, stunning, self-assured woman who took George's breath away. This is not to say that George's past girlfriends were not beautiful and intelligent.

But there was something *different* about Amal. I'll tell you what it was: George found his Dang. Yes, at the age of fifty-three years, George finally met the love of his life, whom he eagerly married.

George was not going to let this remarkable woman get away. There were no endless years of dating. There was no drawn-out engagement. Instead, within eight months from the day George and Amal met, they became husband and wife.

I'm not suggesting eight months as *your* marital timeline. Remember, it all depends upon *your* life goals. Whether it's six months or six years of dating prior to marriage, I want you to stay focused on your life and relationship objectives throughout the process.

Yes, that is how committed love works. There are no doubts, no countless years of dating to determine your compatibility. Doubt means no. Either you Dang, or you don't.

Let's Talk About You

Women know what they want. Why settle for anything less? There are so many wonderful partners out there. If you know you want children, why spend your coin on a man who will rob you of motherhood? If you know you want to be married, why date someone who has not and will not commit to marriage? After a reasonable period of exclusive dating, trust me, he knows you by now. Or let's just say he knows all he needs to know.

At a certain point in your life, it is impractical to give away years to every guy you consider to be your potential committed life partner. Let's say you met "Jason" at the age of thirty-one. Over the course of the next six months, you date Jason exclusively. During those six months, Jason makes it abundantly clear he does not want children. You stay. You hope and pray Jason will see the light and change his mind about children. After all, Jason is insanely handsome and definitely meets your factors of attraction. And, I mean, come on, who would not want to make babies with you, right?

So you give Jason another couple of years of your life. You and Jason move in together. You decorate the apartment. You buy his-and-hers bath towels. By your thirty-third birthday, Jason still has not budged on the issue of children. However, because the sex is great, the apartment rocks, and you two have a ton of fun together, you give Jason a few more years of your life. You are now thirty-five years old. You see where I am going with this, right? Please be prudent with your coin and tell Jason you have decided to invest your money elsewhere.

The Tale of Two Tinas

There are two women I spoke to named Tina, each with a different tale to tell about love. Both Tinas were married at a young age. Both have children, and both marriages lasted well over twenty years. Both Tinas were miserable in their marriages. Outwardly, however, they were both the perfect couples, with beautiful homes, beautiful children, and a wide circle of friends they socialized with as a couple.

Tina Number One

Tina One had an awakening just shy of her thirty-third wedding anniversary. Her kids were grown and living their own lives. Tina spent her entire marriage catering to her children and doting on everyone except herself. Tina had zero interest in her husband. He repulsed her. The thought of sex with him made her cringe, and she avoided intimacy with him at any cost.

Diagnosed with stage 1 breast cancer, Tina began to evaluate her life. She came to the conclusion that she hadn't been living life. Instead, she merely existed. Aside from breathing, there was no life in her. She was just going through the motions. Tina had no passion, excitement, feelings, or emotion. Her life was all a pretense she put on for her community, friends, and family.

One July morning, Tina had an awakening. She'd had enough of her lonely, loveless, sexless life, and she left. She did not take one thing with her except a suitcase full of clothes. Tina, now in her fifties, went to live with her parents and was determined to start a new and fulfilling life. Leaving her marriage was scary, but she never looked back. Tina's children were angry with her. Her husband lashed out and tried to make her life difficult. Her friends took sides.

Through it all, Tina stood her ground and honored her new commitment to herself and her life. She remained focused on her deathbed and the idea of what that moment would have been like, had she stayed in her marriage. Tina thought about how much she had missed out on in life over the past thirty years. Sure, she had had all the material possessions she had always dreamt of. Missing from Tina's life, however, was real love and passion. She had never felt the grip of lusting for her man, and she was determined to find it.

Tina, now living back in the room she grew up in, began to map out her new life. She lived on a mere eight hundred dollars per month that she received in spousal support. Because her children were grown, there was no child support. She went back to school and obtained her real estate license. With time, her children saw happiness emanating from their mother and slowly began to support her decision to leave the marriage.

Tina went skydiving. She took up running. She learned to ski. She started to travel. She hiked the Grand Canyon. She started to come alive. The following year, Tina attended her high school reunion, where she reunited with her long-lost love. Suffice it to say, Tina's new life is now incredibly fulfilling and passionate. I have never seen her happier, and it warms my heart to see such positive energy and new life in every moment she lives.

Tina Number Two

Tina Two has chosen a different life path for herself. Although miserable, Tina has stayed in her marriage and likely always will. Fear of being alone has crippled Tina from leaving her marriage. Fear of change has dictated her fate in life. Financial fear also plays a part in the way Tina has continued to live.

Ten years ago, Tina made the decision to leave her marriage and find a life of passionate love. However, after her first court hearing on support issues, Tina realized she would have to learn to live on less income. Tina decided it would be easier for her if she stayed in her marriage and "sucked it up."

What I hope Tina Two will eventually realize is that *she* holds the key to her happiness. She can (and should) make her own happiness and passion come alive. Complaining about her marriage will not fix her life. Only Tina can make the changes necessary to find and embrace the passion she's missing in her marriage.

For Your Consideration

Consider whether you're better off being alone for a period of time to give yourself the opportunity to find a deepened love. Conversely, if you are content to stay in your current relationship, then that may be your answer.

If you decide to venture into the unknown world of love to find your passion, Don't tell me a year later you should have stayed in misery because you have not yet met anyone. You need to be content with the fact that being single is a better position to be in than in a miserable relationship with a partner you don't want to touch, who never touches you, or to whom you are not sexually attracted. You know as well as I do that you deserve better than that.

I will end this chapter with a recent Facebook post from a friend named Karen:

> *My husband said to me last night:* You are on Facebook all the time. I think you are addicted.
>
> *I am thinking, well, if you would talk to me when you are home this might inspire me not to be on Facebook or reading. But no, you go to bed, turn on Fox News, and then roll over to go to sleep without saying good night. This has been our life for years. No sex. No conversation. No affection of any kind. He has no attraction to me at all and has told me this for years.*
>
> *It is so frustrating to live my life like this. I have voiced my opinion on this behavior when he is home, but every night he goes to bed when he is ready, watches what he wants, and then goes to sleep. No conversation or kiss good night. We have not touched each other in more than two years. Not so much as a kiss. Ugh!*

What would your advice to Karen be?

9

A breakup is your opportunity to create a new masterpiece on the blank white canvas of your life.

The Breakup

Let me start this chapter with one important message: *It's called a "breakup" because it is broken.* Please, remember those words as you navigate your way through Breakup Land.

By now, you should be mindful of your life coin and have started to think about ways to improve your spending habits that will lead you toward your life goals. You have learned about the Dang Factor and its vital, spicy role in creating and maintaining a lasting and mutually loving relationship.

Let's spend some time talking about the dreaded breakup. Maybe you finally realized it was time to leave your loveless and lifeless marriage. Or maybe you've found the courage to quit your never-ending wife audition in order to find a man who is dying to marry you and share a committed life with you.

It doesn't matter if you were on the receiving end of a breakup or the breaker of the relationship. Your role in the breakup is of no consequence. I don't care if he dumped you or you got wise and dumped him (or you are about to dump him). Any way you want to slice the pie, you are now single or about to be single.

As bummed out and pain stricken as you may be, I assure you that you *can* and *will* survive your breakup. In fact, your breakup is an exciting time in your life. Why? Because a breakup is the ideal time to disassemble and rearrange your life. A breakup is the time to grab your life by the nape of the neck and shake things up.

Like a phoenix rising from the ashes, the new you will emerge as a positive and self-assured single woman who knows who she is and what she wants (and does not want) in her future partner; a woman on the cusp of finding what she seeks and living a life filled with adoring love—as long as you are willing to work for it.

If you happen to be reading this book under the covers with a mountain of used tissues and a half-eaten pint of Ben & Jerry's, we've all been there. I'm going to give you a bit of time to mourn the loss of your version of what could have been. However, after a reasonable mourning period, it's time to pick up your paintbrush, walk over to the blank white canvas of your life, and start to create your life masterpiece. Your breakup is the time to harness that heartache into motivation and become the best version of you. And I'm here to help you along the way.

As a general rule, women spend way too much time wallowing in what could or should have been. We tend to spend months, or (gasp!) even years, thinking about our ex and remain paralyzed in disbelief that he found someone else. I mean, how could he, right?

Wrong. You were not his long-term Dang. Or maybe he was not yours. Either way, it does not matter, because as I have told you before, your Dang must be ***reciprocal***. A one-sided Dang is really no Dang at all.

I want you to think of your ex as your guide whose job it was to lead you and light the way to a better way to love. Every ex or breakup you encounter brings you one step closer to finding your soulmate. (Yes, there really is such a thing). In reality, if your partner broke things off, you need to (silently) thank him for the breakup and for the future that awaits you.

If *you* finally broke things off due to his lack of commitment, your ex just did you an incredible favor by stalling or refusing to put a ring on it. I still say a silent thank you to my former men with whom I broke things off for various reasons. Had they not been jerks or had commitment phobia, heaven forbid, I may have married one of them. That would have been tragic, because I would never have met and married my current husband.

In this chapter, I am going to share my "wake-up" story with you as we dissect a breakup from every angle.

Scenes from a Breakup

As much as I would love to get creative and come up with many different scenes for our breakup screenplay, there really are only two scenes in our play:

Scene One: You Broke It Off

Scene Two: He Broke It Off

Sounds pretty simple, right? Wrong. Both scenes from a breakup have many sub-scenes that I want to talk with you about.

Scene One: You Broke It Off

In Scene One, *you*, for whatever reason, made, or are about to make, the decision to end your relationship. Hopefully, you have absorbed the importance of protecting your life coin and have vowed to stop spending precious pennies on your guy. There are many worthy reasons for a Scene One breakup:

- You caught him cheating for the third time.
- You finally realized that your family, friends, and coworkers were right: You two had no future together.

- You recognized he wasn't your Dang after years of living without sexual fireworks or even a spark of desire.
- You understood he was never going to commit and just wanted to keep his dating options open.
- You are in your thirties, and he *still* does not want to start a family.
- You finally had enough after an eight-year audition to be his wife (and still no proposal).
- You realized you have been giving away far too much milk for free and he was never going to buy the beautiful livestock.
- Or maybe, just maybe, you finally realized he was a jerk, and you were never going to change him.

So now what?

I'm a big believer in taking a time out following a breakup. I encourage you to have no contact for at least sixty days. Hang a calendar on your bedroom wall and count out sixty days. Get through each day, second by second if need be, and put a big red "X" through each no-contact day on the calendar.

For the first two months, limit the contact with your now ex. Now, of course, I prefer zero contact, but if you need to arrange child visitation schedules and the like, please keep it short and in an email or text. Bear in mind that each and every time the two of you have contact—and yes, texting and sex count as contact—you move back to an emotional connection with him.

An emotional connection to *him* will keep *you* from moving forward in your new journey.

The Check-Out

My favored breakup scenario entails the woman's (your) mentally, emotionally, and physically "checking out" of the relationship. The "Check-Out" breakup is easy breezy. The beautiful thing about women is the fact that, in a relationship, we will put up with a lot of crap for insanely long periods of time. Women tend to have that bit of "I can change him and make him a better person" way of thinking. Because women think this way, we can (and will) go on for years and tolerate the massive amounts of bullshit our partners often subject us to.

However, the fortunate thing is that once we have had enough of the bullshit, we check out of the relationship. By checking out, I mean we *permanently* check out of the relationship in every way: physically, emotionally, and mentally. There is nothing, and I mean nothing, that can make us check back in.

Once we're checked out, a numbness of emotion takes over our being. Once checked out, a woman will naturally feel no emotional or sexual ties to her ex. A checked-out woman has an easy time moving forward in life. Men, on the other hand, have the innate ability to simply check in and out of the relationship based on their sexual needs at the time. Fortunately for most of us women, when we are done, we are done with every morsel of our beings.

The Wake-Up

If you do not happen to fall into my preferred mode of breakup ("The Check-Out"), the second best scenario for your breakup is "The Wake-Up." In this sub-scene, you finally come to realize your coin has been spent on a partner who is not on the same life path as you are.

In this scene, you come to realize that to achieve your relationship and life goals, you need to end your current relationship. In this scenario, you realize you have auditioned long enough for the starring role as his wife, and it's time to shop for a better-fitting dress. This scene may also come to life when you realize you have been in a relationship that is not a good fit for you and your fabulous future. Now, how are you going to go about closing the current dead-end chapter of your life? Simple. You just do it, and here's how:

First, never give your man an ultimatum. Men do not react well to ultimatums, and you will come off looking desperate (which, of course, you are not). Do you really want to threaten someone into making a commitment to you? Of course not. Stop trying to convince him you are the catch of the century. You (and I) know you are, and that's all that matters.

Remember: This has nothing to do with him. Your enlightenment is only about what will work for *you* and your life goals. Now is the time to take control of your life and forge your path home. The old saying, "It's not you, it's me," is true.

Your partner's behavior (e.g., lack of commitment to you, serial cheating, different life path) is outside your canoe. What is in your canoe is how *you* react to his behavior.

If your reaction to his behavior is to move on with your life and find a partner who cannot wait to make you his wife and the mother of his children, then here you go:

"Kevin, I love you very much (*if, in fact, you do*), but after dating you exclusively for four years, our current situation is not working for *me*. (*Remember, this has nothing to do with him. It's all about* you *and what* you *are willing to live with on your path to achieving your life and love objectives.*) I think it is best that we go our separate ways and date other people so we can both find what we are looking for in a life partner."

And there you have it. No tears. No begging. No groveling. No theatrics. Just say the bare facts spoken in a friendly and calm manner. Peacefully and gently, take the heat for the situation that no longer works for *you*.

Do you see how you gave him no ultimatum for marriage or children? This is all about *you* and what works for *you*. Notice how your words did not put him on the defensive. Do you see the difference between what I recommend versus saying, "If you don't propose to me, I'm leaving you"? (*No one likes a threat, and you are much too classy to intimidate your man into a commitment.*)

Now, after you calmly make your fabulous proclamation to your man, check out his reaction. If he breaks into a panic attack at the mere thought of possibly living life without you, you just *might* have a future with him. If he asks you for some time, give it to him. However, without mentioning it again, you must have a timeline in your mind and stick to it. Don't let him in on the timeline, and do be aware of your coin's being spent day by day. Ultimately, only you can decide how long you are willing to wait for him.

If you make your proclamation, you need to mean it. Do not say it just to gauge his position about his feelings for you. So far, his lack of action on the issue of commitment has been your answer. Anyone can say he wants a future with you. Acting on it and making it happen are two entirely different things. The power to decide and control *your* future should rest in *your* hands, not his.

Once you make your proclamation, you need to be ready for the fallout. I do not ever want to hear from you such regretful statements as "Well, at least I was with *someone*," or "He was better than being alone." You were with a partner who was stalling to see if someone better came along for him to commit to. You were with someone who would not make a commitment and was spending *your* life coin way too freely. (And no, giving him another two years of your life and increasing his blow jobs from once a week to three times per week is not going to change the fact that he has no intention of making a lifetime commitment to you.)

I refuse to believe you would rather stay in a non-fulfilling dead-end situation than move forward and explore life. For every day you choose to stay with a partner who is unwilling to commit or to whom you have no attraction, you give up another day of finding real and reciprocal love with someone else.

I want you to be strong and diligent when it comes to your future. Don't be lazy about love. It's your life, and I want you to take control and be the captain of your own ship. If he wants you to be his wife, he will make a move within a reasonable amount of time. If he wants to start a family with you, he will do that within a reasonable amount of time.

Remember: Men can make babies well into their eighties. Women cannot.

If you do break it off, you can always get back together. I'm not ruling out that possibility for you. However, he knows where you live, and unless he's pounding on your front door on bended knee (ring in hand, of course), then I suggest you move forward with your life and spend your coin more efficiently.

Ending your relationship is not going to create instant happiness. Don't make the mistake of thinking it's going to be all rainbows and butterflies after you walk away from a dead-end situation. You will likely be hurting for some time (provided you had not "checked out" years before). You need to go through the hurt to get over the hurt.

There comes a point in your life when no answer is your answer, and it's time to end the relationship. This could be one of those times.

My Story

My story falls under the "Wake-Up" category. In the four years following my divorce, I had spent my coin on a few, shall we say, *interesting* men. I had my wake-up when my friend told me to "date like a dude" and stop committing so much of my life to one marginal guy. Fortunately, I had already had my children during my first marriage, so I could afford to give away four years when I became single at age forty-four.

After four (fun) years of the single life, I met my true love at the age of forty-eight. It just so happened that my Dang was an airline pilot. Approximately six months into our pretty awesome relationship, my pilot got a career upgrade to captain. The upgrade required him to leave California and go to Louisville, Kentucky, for six months of training.

When it came time for him to leave, he adoringly told me how wonderful it was that I would be waiting for him to complete his training over the next six months. He was so excited to be able to "Skype date" while he was away. Wait. What? Did he just say that? Did he think I was going to put my love life on hold for six months and wait for him to return from training? Why, yes he did!

I was not willing to do that. With my newfound "date like a dude" dating mentality, I realized I would have been nuts to wait around for a guy for six months who had made no long-term commitment to me. In fact, I could have loyally waited for him for six months, and in the meantime, he could have met a new woman in Louisville. That would have meant I gave away an entire year of my life to a guy who had not truly made a commitment to us.

Without batting an eye, and sincerely from the bottom of my heart, I calmly and nicely told my handsome pilot, "I won't be waiting for you during training. You're free to date whomever you like during the next six months, and I'll do the same. Give me a call when you return to California. If we're both single, maybe we can start up where we left off."

It was not an ultimatum. It was not a lecture. It was not a days-long conversation about a commitment. I didn't mention marriage. It was not to gauge his commitment to me. I was merely telling my man what would work for *me*. And I meant it. My words to him had nothing to do with *him*. His initial position was clear when he suggested we Skype date for the next six months. My position was just as clear: That arrangement would not work for *me*.

My man was set to leave for training in one week. The night after I made my position on absentee dating known, we went out to a dinner party. When we returned home, my guy suddenly dropped down to one knee. With a handmade ring, he asked me to marry him. We married two days later at the local courthouse. Three days later, my new husband left for Louisville for six months. I was now more than willing to commit to his training and our newly devoted life together.

I am not suggesting this would be the scenario for you in the same situation. It just so happened I was The One, and he was not about to risk losing me. He took action, and the rest is history. Yes, it really is that simple.

Scene Two: He Broke It Off

In Scene Two of our breakup screenplay, *he* ended the relationship.

Yes, he told you he loved you. You met his family. You talked about a future together. That trip you took together to Italy was magical. You even shared a dog named "Fluffy." And now it's over.

I'll repeat it until I'm blue in the face: for a Dang to be dynamic, it has to be *mutual*. He needs to Dang you just as much or more than you Dang him. A lopsided Dang will not last for the long haul.

I'm not suggesting your ex did not love you at one time. Nor am I suggesting you were not a cool chick whom he liked to hang out with. You just weren't his long-term choice for a wife or mother of his children. And you know what? It's okay. You're going to come away from this breakup better than ever. Thank goodness he dumped you, or ten more years could have gone by before you got this incredible opportunity to reinvent and rebirth yourself and find (your real) "The One."

I promise you, in no time at all, you'll be looking back at your past relationship and shuddering that you stayed in it for so long.

Your breakup is the perfect time to use this newfound singleness as an opportunity to change your life, to reinvent yourself, so to speak; to change and improve something about *you*. Not only does this serve to make you a happier, more well-rounded and fun person, but it's also an excellent distraction.

When I see you next, I want to hear you tell me, "__________ is the reason I learned to surf." (You can fill in the name. Just this one time, I will allow you to refer to him as "Asshole.") Or, "__________ is the reason I finally took that new job in Chicago that I'd wanted for years." How about, "__________ is the reason I finally got serious about my health." "__________ is the reason I got back into snow skiing, something he refused to do with me," sounds fantastic too.

You get the picture. Reinvent yourself. Take classes. Read more. Expand your circle of interests. Join some clubs. Start a new hobby. Travel more. Rearrange your life and savor every new day. Make *you* a priority.

How about taking this time to learn to golf, surf, or ski? Why not return to school and prepare for a career you love? How about volunteering at a local shelter or hospital? Now is the time to redirect your energy toward life-changing strategies. There are abundant opportunities for you to explore, and a breakup is the perfect time to do it. Oh, and if true love finds you along the way, it's a beautiful bonus!

Healing

There are many stages of healing during a breakup. It's natural to take three steps forward and two steps backward during the breakup process. One minute you might feel so positive about your future without him, and the next minute you wonder how you'll survive. I promise: You *will* survive. You must trust the process and the reasons for the breakup.

For your relationship to thrive, both partners must love equally. Non-reciprocated love is not love. In a healthy relationship, both parties share the same feeling of bliss. In a thriving partnership, neither party dumps the other when he or she feels someone better has come along.

What you need and deserve is a partner who loves every inch of you and would give up the world for you. The way your ex handles a breakup is outside your canoe. You can control only what is within your canoe. Anything outside of it—that is, someone else's behavior and actions—you cannot control. The control you *do* have is your *reaction* to his behavior.

The reaction I want from you is to grow from this. Your reaction will be to not give yourself to a partner who steers the relationship on *his* terms. Your reaction is going to be to see the warning signs early on and, when a partner chooses to put you at a distant second in his life, to swiftly realize he is not the partner for you. Your reaction is going to be to learn to love on *your* terms.

I understand breakups hurt. In fact, most breakups downright suck. I never want to minimize the pain you feel after a relationship comes to an end. But I'm here to assure you that it will get better and you will be thriving within a short time. Remember, when a relationship ends, it is because something was broken and the bond between you was not all that healthy or committed. (Otherwise, you'd still be together.)

Inner Peace

Your breakup mission is to be at peace. That being said, I understand he may be a world-class asshole. I get it. I have felt it. He met someone he liked better than you. I understand you were there for him when he needed you. I get the fact that he cheated on you and cleaned out your bank accounts. He's the very definition of a complete jerk. I by no means want to downplay what a creep he turned out to be. However, I do not want you to allow *him* the power to halt *your* future love because of the resentment you feel toward him.

To move forward, we need peace: beautiful, calming, cleansing, accepting, inner peace. If you continue to feel long-term resentment post-breakup, your future will likely never move past where you left off after the split. Make a conscious effort to not let your ex take up space in your brain. If your ex is not paying rent in your head, do not let him live, rent-free, in your thoughts.

The path to inner peace will be a game changer. Yes, he was a complete ass. Yes, he was a cheater, a liar, and an all-around piece of crap. Yes, you want revenge and hope that he will never be happy again. But we women are better than that. And we are too strong to allow our annoyance at him to ruin our future happiness.

As hard as it can be at times, we must take some responsibility for the part we played in the breakup of our prior marriage or relationship. We need to look in at the possibility that we may not have been the best wife or partner that we could have been. We need to be able to recognize when the timing of a relationship is not right and find peace with mistakes we have made and the self-betterment that will come from those past mistakes.

10

With the right partner, sex is one hell of a powerful pleasure.

The Power of Sex

Sex. Think about it. Sex is something so powerful that it has brought down presidents and politicians and made the merely famous infamous. While your lovemaking may not be creating worldwide headlines, never underestimate the sway of sex in your life. I want you to realize the power of sex in your relationship. Quite possibly, you've never really understood the power sex has over your life.

It all starts with the Dang Factor. Meet your match, and the sex comes easily. With your Dang Factor in place, you'll actually crave intimacy with your partner. An entirely new world of sexual feeling will be felt within your body. With the wrong partner, you're just trying to force the love of sex upon yourself. To enjoy it, you need to be attracted to the man you're making love to. It's that simple.

Women are different from men. We need that big slice of Dang to bring out our sexual lioness. We need to feel that something special that makes us tingle in all the right places. When you are with the right partner, you will love, embrace, and have fun with sex. And most of all, you will *have sex*! And it will be satisfying and delightful. Regular intimacy is the glue to your relationship. Men need sex and—guess what?—you do too.

Now don't get me wrong. There are going to be those times when you are so upset or frustrated with your partner, you want to wring his neck. Like any couple, you'll have your ups and downs. There will be amazing days and days where, frankly, you can't stand him. During trying times, sex is the *last* thing on your mind. Trust me, I know. Welcome to couplehood! There may also be medical issues going on that are not conducive to sex during a particular period in your life. However, in the right relationship, you should still crave some closeness with your partner on a fairly regular basis, whether it's touching, cuddling, hugging, kissing, handholding, caressing, walking arm in arm, or some pleasurable combination of these.

I have women tell me all the time that they are not interested in sex. Guess what? For twenty-five years of my first marriage, neither was I. I hated sex. I did anything and everything to get out of having sex with my husband. And now, ten years into my second marriage, I crave sex, as much as, if not more than, when we first started dating. (I know it sounds crazy, but it's true. I can hardly believe it myself!)

The Rubber Band Theory

Think of sex in your relationship like this: Your sexual relationship with your partner is like a rubber band. Every day that passes without intimacy or affection causes your sexual rubber band to stretch out farther. When you go days, weeks, or even months without touch, the rubber band begins to lengthen. As the band lengthens, you start to lose the tight, physical connection you need as a couple. If you allow your rubber band to stretch out too far, it will break. And a broken rubber band is useless.

It's important to keep your relationship from turning into a useless, limp, rubber band. Once you and your partner connect with intimacy or physical touch, the rubber band returns to its optimal tightness. Your intimate connection is now sound and healthy. Sex is powerful. Sex is potent. If you're in a relationship that you'd like to preserve, stay aware of the position of your rubber band.

Sex is the reason he is your partner. Sex is the reason he is not your roommate. Sex is the *one thing* that sets him apart from every other male you know. Sex is what distinguishes him from your brother or your best guy friend. Sex is the one and only reason he gets the title of "husband" or "boyfriend." Without sex and affection, he's simply your good pal. That being said, in order for you to want sex, your partner needs to be your Dang. Personally, I could have read about the importance of sex during my twenty-five-year marriage, but nothing could have changed the fact that I would never crave sex with my husband. He was not my Dang, and I could not force a love of sex into that marriage.

My dear friend Carrie has it right. Her husband is most certainly her true love. The problem is, Carrie's husband wants sex more often than Carrie does. Something Carrie told me one evening stuck in my mind: instead of making sex an issue in their otherwise fantastic marriage, she realized that making love to her man simply takes "a mere eight minutes" of her day. The eight minutes Carrie reserves for her husband several times per week are the most important minutes of her week. Although she's not always "in the mood," Carrie's commitment to her husband has kept her twenty-plus-year marriage strong and vibrant.

We need to understand just how powerful sex is in our relationships. A sexually satisfied partner will move mountains for you. If the rubber band is tight, life feels good. Sex (with the right partner) will create a blissful moment in time and carry through to all aspects of your life. It gets even better than that: A sexually content partner whom you've made your priority is putty in your hands.

Two of the men I interviewed for *The Dang Factor* gave me some excellent insight on this very topic. I'm passing it on to you in hopes that you too will learn to make your own putty.

Steve's Story: The Power of the Band

Steve is a handsome forty-five-year-old man who has been married for twenty-one years. Steve confessed to previously having had several affairs, something he isn't proud of. Steve told me about the power his wife would have over him *if only* she *would* have sex with him.

Steve's story is a common one. Steve hates to shop. In fact, Steve despises shopping. Steve's wife loves to shop. Moreover, she loves for Steve to shop *with* her, something Steve has always refused to do. Steve candidly explained the simple thought process in his mind when it comes to shopping, as well as all daily activities in his marriage:

> My wife doesn't understand the power she has over me. If my wife were to eagerly and happily have sex with me, not only would I love to spend time shopping with her, I would whip out my wallet and give her every dollar and credit card I have! Why? Because I'm a happy and satisfied man who feels wanted and loved. In my state of bliss, I would do anything for my wife, and that includes shopping. Instead, I have to beg for intimacy, and I still never get it. If by some off chance we do have sex, I feel guilty because I know she's not into it.

Jack's Story: Why Some Men Cheat

Cheating is an epidemic with a cure. I firmly believe that. My friend Jack does too. Jack gave me his insight on the topic of cheating and the male perspective on why men cheat. Here's what he said.

Jack was married to Alicia for fourteen years. At the beginning of their marriage, Jack was extremely content. He was happy and satisfied and never would have imagined being unfaithful to Alicia. Although there were things about Alicia that bothered Jack, they were minimal in the big picture of marriage. The reason Jack ignored Alicia's bothersome traits was simple: Jack was having regular sex with his wife.

Fast forward a few years into Jack and Alicia's marriage, and things began to dramatically change. Two kids, one dog, three cats, and one horse later, Jack was not having *any* sex with Alicia. All of Alicia's attention went to the children and the pets. Alicia also focused on her friends, her scrapbooking (with pictures of only the kids and the pets), and her horse shows.

I was fascinated as Jack explained the evolution of how his cheating came to fruition. Jack felt everything else was more important to Alicia than he was. On Alicia's list of priorities, Jack was dead last. Getting a simple kiss goodbye had become a chore.

What intrigued me, even more, was the number of times Jack spoke of a simple cup of coffee during our interview. Some twelve years after their divorce, Jack is still hurt by the fact that Alicia would never make him a cup of coffee. Even after a knee surgery, when Jack couldn't walk, Alicia refused to make coffee, telling Jack, "I don't drink coffee." To Jack, that cup of coffee meant more than sipping some morning joe. It meant Alicia cared about him and wanted to do something nice. To Jack, it meant *his* needs were important.

Jack explained how regular sex and a little attention from Alicia would have negated the lack of coffee or Alicia's lack of cleanliness. For closeness, Jack explained, he would gladly hobble over to make his own coffee; but without closeness, the lack of coffee or the pile of Alicia's dirty clothes in the bathroom only served to agitate him. "Who cares about the lack of coffee if I just had sex with my wife?" he said. However, without intimacy, coffee and dirty clothes turned into a big deal.

When sex and thoughtfulness in their marriage were present, Jack focused solely on the positive part of their marriage and never gave the negative part a second thought. That is, until the positive (sex) disappeared and all that remained were the bothersome (in Jack's mind) traits of Alicia.

During our conversation, Jack was adamant about several things:

1. The sexual component in his marriage kept him grounded and focused on his family.
2. Although he was hugely successful in his career,

without sex in his marriage Jack felt unfulfilled and unaccomplished.

3. The sexual aspect of his marriage was of great importance to Jack.
4. Jack would never have cheated had he felt he was a priority in his marriage.
5. The woman Jack cheated with gave Jack the attention he was no longer getting at home.

Jack's story demonstrates just how powerful sex, or the lack of sex, is in your relationship. I want you to visualize your rubber band on a daily basis. I'm not saying you need to have sex every day; far from it. What I am saying is that some form of touch and affection on a regular basis should be present. Do not allow your rubber band to overstretch and snap. Use the power of sex and touch to keep your relationship grounded and solid.

Remember, there is always an exception to every life situation. Jack's cure for the cheating plague will not apply to the serial cheaters we discussed in Chapter 6: The (Cave) Men.

Jessica's Story: When "I Do" Becomes "I Don't"

Jessica's story comes from an online forum I hosted. Jessica's attitude and several of the women's follow-up responses illustrate Jack's point, spot on. Once you stop caring, once your partner is no longer your priority, once you have lost your desire for intimacy, your relationship has entered a dangerous zone. If you feel the way Jessica does, but you still have a morsel of feeling left for your partner, it is important to pull yourself out of this toxic zone and readjust your rubber band back into the proper position.

Jessica wrote:

> *My husband just got home from a work trip last night. I picked him up at the airport and gave him a hug. This morning he is walking around pouting, saying I didn't miss him because I'm not giving him more hugs and kisses.*
>
> *I said, "It's not like I'm not used to you leaving. We've been together for seven years. I'm used to you going and coming. I'm not going to act like some women do every time their man comes home from a work trip and act like it is some sort of big deal, because it's not."*

Once your desire for another is gone, and one or both of you is no longer a priority, that leaves little to cling to at home. And *home* should always be each other's soft place to fall in this hard-ass life.

Using Jack's theory, this is precisely when one or both spouses will start to look elsewhere for desire and attention. In fact, one may not even set out to consciously "look" for attention. One day, as in Jack's case, attention found Jack, and Jack reciprocated.

Sadly, the responses to Jessica's post are equally illustrative of the demise of many marriages. Here are the responses:

> Jennifer: *Tell him to suck it up. I am not lovey like I was in the beginning either. Our life is now very routine and predictable.*

> *I will not sit around pining for him. I will do my thing, and he can do his.*
>
> Bree: *Yeah! Don't kiss his ass! Me wanting to give attention to a man has only happened once, and it was not with my hubby!*
>
> Christine: *My husband can be home a day or two before I even think to kiss him.*
>
> Shelly: *I had a talk with my man. I said, "I can't just drop everything and give you attention when you get home!" There is just no time (or desire) to give him attention, especially sex.*
>
> Janet: *You need to tell him to get over the sentimental and sex stuff.*
>
> Eve: *Well, I don't get anything from him. Why should I give him any attention?*
>
> Madison: *Men are such babies. Mine pouts on a daily basis about not getting any attention or sex! I have no time for him, so he needs to get a grip.*

Don't make the mistake so many couples make in their relationships. The sex is rampant and carefree when you first start dating. However, once you marry, life takes over, your priorities shift, and in no time at all the sexual connection is lost. This is where you not only give up your sexual power, but you scar your connection to your partner. Intimacy, sex, affection, and touch are the most compelling and valuable components of your relationship.

Sex is the glue that cements your relationship as a couple. It's special and sacred to just the two of you. It's a powerful act of union that keeps you centered and connected during the hard times. Don't let yourself fall into the situation of being married to a roommate. You both deserve to experience a love much deeper than brotherly/sisterly love.

Please don't take this chapter out of context. Obviously, a medical condition, sickness, or debilitating illness will not allow for traditional intimacy. Similarly, pregnancy and adjusting to life as new parents are sure to throw a wrench into the sexual works temporarily. With a newborn or a toddler (or both), most parents are lucky to get a high five in. During trying life adjustments (pregnancy, birth, recovery, your period, new parenthood, sickness, and menopause), simply making an effort to have a moment of closeness, touching, or holding hands will help you keep your rubber band tight. The power of touch is a beautiful thing, no matter how it's accomplished.

11

*To find love you must seek love.
To seek love you must announce
your presence to the world.*

Profile Your (Love) Life

So after all of my nagging, if you're single or about to be single, I hope you've decided it's time to get out there and announce to the world you are *single* and *available*! I hope you understand that unless you make finding love a priority in your life, you may very well miss out on the chance to experience and absorb real, feel-it-to-your-toes mutual love.

Trust me; the love of your life is out there. I promise you there's a partner for everyone on this planet. You simply need to make the commitment to find him and, conversely, let yourself be found.

I get frustrated when I see how many of my friends in their thirties, forties, fifties, and sixties have become so lackadaisical and casual about their love lives. I want to scream when I see some of the careless ways many women spend their life coin. Sure, everyone wants to be in love. Some even complain daily about being single.

The problem is, some folks do nothing to make that love happen. I want to shake them by the shoulders and scream, "*You need to do it now, woman!*" (And trust me, sometimes I do.)

Don't leave love to fate. Don't leave it up to God, or to "when the time is right." The time is *now*. If you want to be married, have children, find the love of your life, or experience lust and mutual adoration for your partner, then you need to grab your love life by the nape of the neck and shake it up. I want you to take charge of the direction you're headed and the future you desire. Maintaining your love life is your job, and keeping it fresh will continue to be your job for as long as you live.

Below are a few of my friends' responses to my years of prodding them to start rowing their boat into the harbor of happiness:

> Stacey, age fifty-eight: "*I am focusing on my career right now. In the future, I will get serious about dating.*"
>
> Lauren, age fifty-two: "*Maybe someday, not now. I want to lose some weight first.*"

Lisa, age forty-eight: *"It's way too much work to date!"*

Debbie, age forty-two: *"My kids don't want me to date, so I am going to wait until they graduate college."*

Grace, age thirty-six: *"My ex-husband does not want me to date yet." (Huh?)*

Karen, age thirty-nine: *"There's no point. All the good ones are taken anyway."*

Mary, age forty-four: *"Dating feels weird at my age."*

Tari, age forty: *"I will try to get serious about it later. I am just so busy now."*

Devon, age thirty: *"If it is meant to be, it will be."*

Do you feel my pain? Do you see why I get so upset about the complacent attitude of some of my friends? I want them to find good love. Just like I want you to find good love.

My friend Sophie likes to complain about the fact that she doesn't have a man in her life, yet she does absolutely nothing to find one. Nothing! Does she think an alien is going to just someday drop a man on her doorstep with a note reading, "Sophie, I am the love of your life, and I was sent to your doorstep to spend my life with you"?

In this chapter, as we profile your (love) life, we'll tie up all the loose ends and ultimately change the way you love. This chapter will help put into motion your new career as the certified accountant of your life coin. As *The Dang Factor* comes to an end, you're going to walk away ready to date smart, spend smart, and live smart. Ready?

It's time to chat about one of my favorite things: online dating. (No eye rolls, please.) Online dating is the best invention to have made its way onto our laptops and phones in the past decade. Imagine yourself shopping for your partner, while sitting in your living room sipping a glass of wine. Yes, that is how you can find your future love in the twenty-first century.

Now some of you may be in the small minority who may meet their future love in the produce aisle of Whole Foods—but I wouldn't bet your bananas on it. Why? Because your odds of meeting your future partner on fate alone are simply not in your favor. We live in such a busy society. Our lives are chaotic, and our grocery store runs are purposeful and hurried. Online dating is here to stay and has evolved into the most widely accepted and practical way to date throughout the world. With online dating the new reality, I suggest you pull up a comfy chair so we can get started.

Charge Your Laptop: It's Time for a Lesson on Smart Spending

Dating online isn't magic. It's work, and it takes a lot of effort. You're likely going to go through many dates before your match is found. Or you could be one of the select few who get to experience possible love in their first week of dating. Who knows? Who cares? As long as you're out there looking and making yourself *actively* available, you need to trust the process of finding love.

That is why we call it "dating." Dating means going on dates to see what people are like. Remember the wife audition I talked about in previous chapters? Well, your mutual dating auditions are the only way you're going to find out whether he's your future match.

When I was single and I balked at the idea of online dating, my mother asked me, "How many men came knocking on your door today?" Sheepish, I answered "None." She sternly reminded me it was because no one knew I was available and looking for love. Now, it's my turn to sternly remind you of the same thing.

If you want to find passionate love, then I want you to *go get it!* We women have the power to change our lives; we simply need to take action! No more complaining. From this moment forward, finding your fabulous partner is your second job. Yes, it's work. But it's also exciting to embark on this quest to find your new, fantastic, and life-changing relationship.

You know you're the catch of a lifetime. But how the heck is your future guy going to know how insanely perfect you are for him if you do not make your available self known to the world? From this day forward, you are officially promoted to the "marketing manager" of *your life*. It's time to take charge of the direction of your life and invest in the best stock ever: *You!*

Where do you start? By creating an enticing profile that will highlight who you are. Yes, it has to be enticing. A lot of single women are out there, and you need to stand out. You're selling yourself on a web page as the awesome and (humble) person you are. With a few great pictures and a well-written bio, you'll be on your way to finding the love of your life.

It helps to have a playful attitude as I guide you through the curves of dating. And please don't try to tell me online dating is too expensive. A mere thirty bucks a month for your future is the best investment you'll ever make. If you pack a lunch a couple of times a week or order fewer Starbucks lattes, you have just paid for your online dating bill.

Ground Rules

Let's start with some ground rules for dating:

Rule 1: You Have to Go Through It to Get Over It

Rule 2: Be Realistic in Your Dating Quest

Rule 3: Respect the Gender Roles

Rule 4: Share a Mutual Interest with Any Potential Partner

Rule 5: Give It Time

Now, let's dive in.

Rule 1: You Have to Go Through It to Get Over It

You, my perfect peach, are not exempt from the agony, effort, and disappointment we *all* have to go through to find "The One." You're going to have bad dates. You're going to get emails and winks from weirdoes and creeps. This is where that ability to find a touch of humor in the online dating process comes in handy. However, each bad date or creepy email will lead you one step closer to your future love.

You aren't going to focus on the bad dates and creeps. Instead, you're going to focus on potential matches who just may end up being your life partner. You will likely have to kiss a few frogs before you find your prince. Or, you could be lucky enough to find good love on your first date. We won't know the answer until you jumpstart your quest.

Trust this process. I don't want it to be an easy journey. It's the searching and narrowing down to exactly what you want from your future partner that makes this process work. I want you to feel the pain of some bad dates. I promise, soon you will look back, and it will be clear why there *were* some marginal dates: every bad date led you one step closer to good love.

I need you to get out of your comfort zone and put the time and effort into *your* future. No one will do the dating for you. It's work to date, and you must carve out the time, energy, and effort to make it happen. This means checking your dating profile every day. It entails responding to emails, sending winks, and promoting daily communication between you and your potential dates.

Men are like wet noodles. During this dating journey, picture yourself in your kitchen cooking up a nice big pot of pasta noodles. Think of all the wet noodles as the people you're about to meet on your new venture. Now strain the noodles and throw them all against your kitchen wall. How many stick? One? Two? Exactly! Most will fall to the floor, but I promise you, with time, one or two delicious noodles will stick.

Out of the hundreds of noodles I dated, I met some wonderful men and a few, shall we say, *interesting* men. The majority of the men I dated were not a match for me, but I have remained friends with several of them to this day. Every noodle you meet does not have to be a romantic connection. As long as you cook the pasta, throw the noodles, and put in the effort, one delicious noodle will eventually stick.

Rule 2: Be Realistic in Your Dating Quest

Dating is going to take time and effort on your part. My friend Mary finally heeded my nagging and put herself on Match.com. Mary received many emails, winks, and date requests. I was thrilled for Mary's new venture. The next time I spoke to Mary, I asked her how her dating was going, only to be informed she had canceled her Match.com subscription.

"What?" I shrieked.

"It was not working," Mary explained.

"How long were you on there?" I asked.

Mary answered, "One week."

As you might imagine, I about had a coronary at Mary's idea that one measly week on Match.com was going to result in her finding the love of her life. *Dating takes time.*

You also need to be realistic and date within your means. What is dating within your means? It is dating someone of like kind. It means dating someone with a similar socioeconomic, educational, and life status. Holding out for the next Brad Pitt is impractical unless, of course, you are the next up-and-coming movie star. Having unattainable expectations of your future partner is unrealistic.

If you are a grocery bagger with a high school education and you will date *only* a doctor or lawyer, you are not likely to be successful in your journey for love. You must be realistic about what you bring to the relationship and not limit your dating options to a probable non-option. This is not to say that a bartender cannot marry a famous actor (Matt Damon). However, your odds of such an event are not in your favor.

A good example of an unrealistic dating expectation is my friend Quinn. Quinn has received many date requests from her dating profile. Quinn is a great catch and would make an incredible partner. So what's the problem? Quinn will date *only* a Scorpio. Yes, you read that right. Yes, as in the astrological sign. Quinn has refused even to consider going on a date with an Aquarius, Taurus, or Pisces.

Quinn's rule is neither realistic nor sensible. Quinn's refusal to even consider a Libra or Cancer only serves to cut her dating pool down to one-twelfth of available men. Quinn will also not consider dating anyone under 6'4". Quinn has remained adamant: a 6'2" Libra will not even be considered for a partner. Quinn's chances of finding her love are extremely limited, if not nonexistent.

Rule 3: Respect the Gender Roles

During the dating process, men generally want a bit of a caveman challenge. Frankly, women tend to be turned off by the too available and pushy guys as well. We all like a bit of a challenge in love and life. I'm not advocating that you play games by any means. But I am suggesting that you let the man assume the male role in the dating process. You can, of course, make the first move to get his attention. You can initiate the initial flirting and first connection. However, once he has your contact information, I highly recommend you let him court you.

One of the biggest complaints from the thousands of men I interviewed was that their male role in society had been undermined and diminished over the years. Once he has your contact information, he knows how to get in touch with you. And if you get no answer, well, that's your answer. Being too available and (gasp!) too needy is strictly forbidden. Please resist the urge to chase. Remember, the egg sits still. The fish swim.

Rule 4: Share a Mutual Interest with Any Potential Partner

My fourth ground rule is for you to have something in common with your potential partner. I was guilty of breaking this rule during my first marriage. My ex and I had absolutely nothing in common—and no, children do not count as a common interest. Mutual interests keep you connected as a couple.

In my present marriage, it is incredible how much closeness and affection comes from simply having mutual interests. It is like being married to your best friend, with the bonus of sex. Together, my partner and I travel, surf, ski, work out, run, wine taste, and explore life, as a tag team. If you spend months or years *trying* to convert your potential mate to have the same interests as you, that is precious time that could be spent with someone who instinctively shares your hobbies.

Rule 5: Give It Time

I promise online dating does work. I do *not* promise an instant love fest, because you know as well as I do that real love will take time to find. I don't want you to put a timeline on finding good love. So what if it takes six months or even six years to find "The One"? There are no shortcuts or free passes to love. Keep your profile active, and maintain a positive dating attitude. Don't let a few bad dates detour you.

Your Dating Profile

Now that I've convinced you to go online to expand your opportunities for finding love, it's time to get started. Match.com is a great place to start your new online adventure. Some other dating sites offer you more specific targeted potential matches, for example, Christian, athletic, or over fifty. There is also Tinder and Bumble for your dating pleasure. Those sites can be useful if you have specific criteria you are after. I suggest you take the first, big step and start with the basic Match.com profile.

The Basics

Men are visual beings. Men will not likely take the time to absorb the life story you have so beautifully written on your dating profile. The best rule of thumb is to keep it simple.

So what is your future partner looking for when skimming dating profiles? First and foremost, they're looking at your profile picture and checking out your energy. Does she like to have fun? Is she a positive person who is adventurous and low maintenance? Is she the opposite of his past relationship where the arguing overpowered the love? Does she appear to be someone who will enhance his life rather than complicate it? (Of course, you're assessing the same qualities in your potential mate as well!)

As you create your profile, remember your audience. Most men on a dating site are starting over in their quest for love. A good majority will be fresh out of a breakup or divorce. Less is more at this first stage of dating. Remember, you are marketing *you* in this profile.

I estimate at least 80 percent of men on most dating websites are interested in marriage or remarriage. Remember: Most men love to be married. The key, of course, is that, if you are marriage minded, each of you ultimately meets your respective Dang criteria.

Your Photos

I cannot stress enough the importance of a great profile picture. Your profile picture is your first (and possibly only) chance to impress. We are visual beings. Your profile picture needs to be visually appealing. No mirror selfies. No hats, no sunglasses. A beautiful smile is contagious. Happiness is attractive.

Make certain your profile picture is of you and you alone. Don't crop people out of your pictures. Take the time to find a few photos of just you. For the additional photos, limit the number to a maximum of six pictures. Leave your kids, friends, and exes out of the pictures. (One picture with your doggie is allowed.) Post photos of your being active and enjoying life—surfing, dog walking, skiing, snowboarding, toasting with a glass of wine. Oh, and go easy on the cleavage. A little is fine. A lot is too much. Leave something to the imagination.

Your Dating Headline

Most dating sites require an identifying headline as part of your dating profile. Your headline is an important part of your dating profile, and it will be read. Your headline is a short phrase that describes you or your outlook on life. Keep your headline upbeat. If you have a particular sport or hobby you enjoy, you may want to use that as a headline. If you enjoy the beach, a catchy beach phrase is a good start. Think about what makes you an amazing person to get to know. The possibilities are endless.

Headlines to avoid (yes, these are actual headlines; my responses are in parentheses):

"Megan's Mommy" *(He is not looking for a mommy. He has one.)*

"Into Cash" *(Really?)*

"Hopeful in San Diego" *(Sounds desperate.)*

"Your Princess" *(He does not want a princess. Been there. Done that.)*

"Be HONEST" *(No need to advertise your last guy was a liar.)*

"Marriage Minded" *(Slow down, Cowgirl! All in due time.)*

"NCYFEIT" *(What the hell does this even mean?)*

"CAVPA318" *(Please, no vanity plates that no one can figure out.)*

"Can I Find Just One Decent Guy?" *(Sounds too negative.)*

Your Written Profile

With a few great pictures and an enticing headline, your profile (if not too long) *will* be read. So keep your bio to no more than three to four short paragraphs. A few paragraphs about you will help pique the interests of your potential dates. If they notice mutual interests or find something about you intriguing, this will be a starting point for your communication.

Keep your profile confident, uplifting, and lighthearted. Be a breath of fresh air. I want your profile to radiate positivity. Evoke optimistic energy. Be ready for a fresh start and an incredible rest of your life!

Exes and children should remain a minimal topic of conversation in the beginning. You can talk about the children and integrate them into the equation if you progress as a couple. Until then, keep the focus on the two adults. I'm not saying you can't talk about your children on your first date. Of course you can. However, your life and your dating profile should not be a living testament to your three kids.

Make sure you're both looking for the same outcome before diving into endless dates with someone. If his profile says he does not want kids, he likely means it. If his profile says he will not remarry, the chances are he means it. If his profile says he doesn't want to date someone who has kids, he means it. Pay attention to his profile. You don't want to spend your precious coin trying to change his mind.

I have a male friend who has been on Match.com for twelve years. Twelve years! He has no intention of getting married and is what I call a "serial dater." You may come across a few serial daters on your journey. Pay attention to the warning signs. Don't get dragged into a dating bubble you can't pull away from.

Your dating profile is your life résumé, and your résumé needs to rock.

Now, let's look at a few sample (and real) profile *"Dos and Don'ts."*

"Independent Warrior"

(Although I applaud her independence, this headline is too strong. You don't want to appear as if you don't need or want a partner in life. Too much warrior in you is more of a turn-off than a turn-on. A softer approach to show you are independent and driven would be better in the body of your profile.)

I am a full-time parent of my sixteen-year-old son, who plays water polo. He is my life. My son is really important and comes first, over everything. Athletic activities are exciting, and my lifestyle is very sports oriented. I am a loyal Angels, Kings, and Lakers fan. If these are not your teams, please don't contact me.

(This "Independent Warrior" is not likely to get much response from her dating profile. First off, Mr. Wonderful does not want to compete for her time with her sixteen-year-old son. Remember, your potential mate likely came from a relationship where he

dropped to dead last in the pecking order of attention. Of course, our children are important and a top priority; however, you need to make sure your love life also stays in the top tier of your priorities. Secondly, although her love of sports is a good thing, her "Don't contact me" attitude is not. Why would you want to limit your dating possibilities? A Padres fan or a Knicks fan could very well be your Dang.)

"No Time for This"

(This headline sounds impatient and agitated.)

Oh my God! How much crap do I have to fill out to get signed up for this website? Okay, people!!! What's with the no picture thing??? I took the time to upload pictures. You can do the same thing!

I am not looking for anything serious. I am just bored and looking for friends to kill some time with. Send me an email and let me know when you want to meet up.

(I swear, this is a real profile. Please pay attention as to how your written words read to a potential partner. Although probably written in a joking fashion, the words do not come across as funny. Believe it or not, most men are looking for something serious. Again, keep your options open.)

"Are You the One for Me?"

(This headline is not too shabby. Unfortunately, she will not likely find the answer to her question based on her profile.)

I want a guy who wants to spend his time with me and will respect and encourage me to the fullest. I have three wonderful kids to whom I devote my time, so you *must* love my kids. I'm not into guys who think too highly of themselves, so please take it down a notch if you want to date me.

(Things like respect and encouragement will come along as the relationship progresses. Demanding respect in the first sentence of your profile sounds, well, demanding. Again, easy does it on the kid announcement. Kids are great. Making demands regarding your children is not great. Lastly, let's face it: most guys think highly of themselves. A demand to "take it down a notch" will brutally limit your dating pool.)

"Adventurous, Down to Earth, and Fun Loving!"

(What's not to like in this headline? It's perfect. As you read this profile, you will see why this is one of my favorites. This profile has such a "feel good" vibe to it. The author is laid back and undemanding, and, frankly, she sounds like someone any guy would have a ton of fun spending time with and getting to know.)

I am a laid back woman who is close to her family and friends. I'm a native of San Diego but love Chicago, where the majority of my family still lives. I love adventure, travel, and spontaneity, especially when my snowboard is with me! Staying in for a movie and snuggling is nice too!

I'm looking for someone I can share these experiences with. I work hard in my career so I can play hard on my time off. You will find me on the slopes during winter and wakeboarding and enjoying the outdoors the rest of the time. I do like to get dressed up now and then too! Let's have some fun!

My Favorite Spots Around Town:

Love the food in Little Italy and the intimate settings. La Jolla Shores, Encinitas, and dive bars are great too.

My Favorite Things:

Winter is my time of the year; snowboarding is my passion. In my free time, you'll find me at CorePower Yoga, running, at CrossFit, or enjoying a movie. I do yoga about four to five days a week. It's great for mind, body, and soul! I hope you will join me!

Last Thing I Read:

Living Your Yoga

"VIP Woman"

(Let him be the judge of your VIP status. This next profile is my all-time "Do Not Do This" profile. As you compare these two profiles, notice the difference between not only the written words but also the tone of each profile. Remember your audience. You are posting your life résumé for the purpose of finding your

future partner. You need to sound and be positive, upbeat, and non-demanding.)

Relationship Status: Never married, forty-eight years old

Have kids: No

Wants kids: Yes

THIS is what I'm searching for:

Although one of my favorite TV channels is SPEED, let me share that I'm very much a girlie girl. You *must* be a manly man. I have a Southern soul and spirit along with a huge heart. Very much enjoy laughing as it "feeds" me, and as for the man who wins my heart, I'll be laughing either "with" him or "at" him! No drama here and I do not want any of your drama.

I am fiercely loyal, driven, honest, intelligent, and loving, and I know exactly what I want. Not looking to play the field or juggle countless dates but looking for ONE honest, stimulating, and deep relationship. I will not waste my time on someone who does not add to my life.

I am looking for a "masculine" man. To be wrapped in your arms would be the warmest and safest place in the world. Please take notice: Your arms *must* be large. You *must* be someone who instantly catches my eye, yet will also have that "extreme" intelligence and chemistry that turns my mind on. Again, you *MUST* be intelligent or do not message me. You *must* light my fire. Yet, I will still love your perfect imperfections! My man *must* be HONEST, driven, confident, strong, masculine, witty, exciting, and funny. You also *must* have interests. You *must* be financially on the high earning side, and you *MUST* own your own home! You will also be dripping of personality and charisma!

Do not lie about your age. You *must* be over your last relationship. Do not waste my time if you are not. Again, you *must* be intelligent. Delete those silly photos in front of a mirror. They are not attractive. Delete those photos with a woman on your lap. They are not attractive. Lastly, I am not looking to date your Corvette or motorcycle, so take those pictures down.

(Be humble. Be nice. Step back and ask how you are coming across on your life résumé. Making demands is not going to get you where I want you to be. I want you to find, feel, and experience the best love of your life. Crafting the right profile is just the first important step in your journey to good love.)

One More Profile

As we wrap up drafting your dating profile, I am going to leave you with my all-time favorite Match.com profile! Okay, I'll admit, this was my dating profile, which I used on Match.com, and I want to share it with you. Why? Because it worked. My profile led me (after a significant number of soggy noodles) straight to the absolute love of my life.

Sure, I had to get down in the dating trenches for five years and find my way out, but the result has been magnificent! I paid my dues. I put the time in. During those five years, I had some bizarre dates and some strange relationships. But all the bad dates and weirdness led me to my beloved husband. Don't ever give up. Your love is out there, waiting to be found.

"Friendship on Fire!"

(This headline is fun, light, and catchy. To have a friendship catch on fire is a beautiful thing.)

A few things about me: I am affectionate, playful, soulful, and fun. I love life, staying active, fitness, surfing, skiing, travel, new adventures, slow dancing together in the kitchen, cooking together, great conversation, toasting before our first sip, snuggling up for a movie, amazing talks, fabulous walks, incredible sunsets, and seizing the moment!

A few things about you: You are a man who works hard, plays harder, and lives and loves passionately. You have strong family values and a thirst to live life and enjoy love. And, you are ready to experience an incredible rest of your life.

My Favorite Places:

Tropical places for travel and surfing... lots of sand, surf, and sunshine. Exploring life and savoring every moment of it!

A Few of My Favorite Things:

Good food, good wine, and great company. Savoring life's best moments! You know, those times that just stick in your mind forever and still make you smile when you think about them years later.

Last Thing I Read:

Outside My Boat

Throughout life, it is important to recognize the things that are definitely outside of our control.

My Idea of a Great Date:

Let's meet for a glass of wine or a cup of coffee and get to know each other!

12

Analyze your life. Undo your life. Reshuffle your life. Begin your life.

The Beginning

With this last chapter of *The Dang Factor* begins the first chapter of *you.* My sisters, please never give up on mutual and adoring love. Life could surprise the hell out of you one day, and you might just wake up one morning and find yourself smack dab in the middle of paradise.

Above all else, remember this: To find something you have never had, you need to do something you have never done. Take a chance. Walk outside of your comfort zone. Shake things up. Disassemble and rearrange your life. Go find your Dang.

Resurrect your Dang. Walk away from bad love and make good love happen!

I wrote *The Dang Factor* because I want women everywhere to know they are in charge of their own lives and the direction their lives ultimately take. I wrote *The Dang Factor* because I want my sisters to know I have their backs and to take my hand as we analyze not only the "Dang Factor" in their past, current or future relationships, but most importantly, to never allow a bad date, a breakup, a betrayal, or a divorce to define *their* future.

I'm not going to pretend to know the outcome of your life if you do set out to seek your Dang or rekindle your love. You won't know the outcome, unless and until you venture out to make good love happen. I *do*, however, know the outcome of your life if you *don't* set out to find the missing link of your life.

Since the passing of my father, my life and, more importantly, my impending deathbed, have come full circle. What I once envisioned as a regretful and saddened moment that was missing the link of mutual and true love has transformed itself into a moment of complete satisfaction. I will take solace knowing that during my lifetime I have loved to the deepest level on earth. I found the "Dang Factor" that had been missing from my life, and I never want you to miss out on your chance at finding the missing piece to your heart's puzzle.

Deathbed, ladies, deathbed! Make it a good one.

Acknowledgments

A huge thank you to Alfredo, for his unwavering support and encouragement throughout my journey to discovering love. You are the soul of *The Dang Factor*.

Thank you to my beautiful children and my incredibly supportive mother for understanding and loving my passion for life and love. I adore you all.

I cannot express enough thanks to my incredible team of women who not only encouraged and guided me through the process of bringing this book to life, but also became my dear friends along the way. Jeniffer Thompson, thank you from the bottom of my heart.

Lastly, and most importantly, thank you to my father for providing me with one of life's greatest lessons: We have the power to disassemble and rearrange our lives. We have the power to change the way we love.

The second book in

THE FACTOR SERIES®

The Dude Factor is a straightforward and simple lesson—for men only—on preserving the Dang Factor phenomenon and living a life filled with damn good love.

The Dude Factor is a man's guide to *The Dang Factor* and speaks to men about sex, nurturing, commitment, communication, and how to be an overall good dude.

A refresher course on love, *The Dude Factor* will chart your path to relationship longevity and satisfying love.

An advocate of Good Love. As a divorce attorney for more than twenty years, Michelle has witnessed firsthand the *reasons* more than 50 percent of marriages fail in the United States. Previously married for twenty-five years, Michelle decided, after hearing her father's deathbed confession, to leave her marriage and seek a deep love she had never experienced. Michelle's five-year journey led her to discover a life phenomenon called "The Dang Factor," where, for the first time in her life, she felt adoring and sexual love.

As part of the extensive research for *The Dang Factor* and *The Dude Factor*, Michelle personally conducted more than 4,000 interviews. She spoke with 2,000 men and 2,016 women about the topics found in both books. From sex and betrayal to dating and divorce, no topic was off limits. From the young and the old, to the rich and the poor, these men and women, both single and married, revealed their hearts and souls to Michelle. Unfiltered and real, Michelle represents men and women everywhere. But more importantly, she speaks the truth of discovering and preserving damn good love!

Made in the USA
San Bernardino, CA
17 September 2018